Praise for The Cross Worked.

In *The Cross Worked.*, Zach Maldonado shatters common religious misconceptions about God and shines a bright spotlight on the Christian message. He offers us a depth and a clarity that are rarely found in Christian teaching today. This book is both powerful and liberating, and in its pages you'll discover the truth that really does set you free!

- Dr. Andrew Farley, bestselling author of *The Naked Gospel*, and host of Andrew Farley LIVE on Sirius XM AndrewFarley.org

Zach Maldonado is a young hero of mine. He is intolerant of any hint of theology that ties new covenant believers into doubt, shame or fear. Here, he builds a compelling argument of a salvation that cannot be unraveled. If it sounds familiar it's because Scripture, without a man-made, moralistic filter, presents the same assurance. I'm so proud to know this passionate, articulate defender of our identity in Christ.

- John Lynch, Pastor, Speaker, and Coauthor of *The Cure*

Zach Maldonado has brought together many of the most important truths of the gospel of Jesus Christ and expressed them beautifully. There are very few books that do that as well as this one, so please don't miss "The Cross Worked."!

- **Ralph Harris**, author of *God's Astounding Opinion of You*, President of LifeCourse Ministries.

I can't say enough good things about Zach Maldonado. Not only is he a close friend, he is an incredible voice in this generation. His passion for everyone to find the freedom and confidence only found in the completed work of the cross shines through in this book. Too often we only believe the cross accomplished enough to get things started for us. The title, The Cross Worked. , ends with a period for a reason. In this book, Zach unpacks the eternal and ultimate confidence this period promises us through the beautiful gift of the New Covenant.

- **Chad Belew,** Lead Pastor at the Arsenal Church, San Antonio, Texas

So many Christians embrace the forgiveness of God offered in the grace of the Lord Jesus through His work on the cross, yet continue to live in guilt, shame, and fear that God is still going to judge them for their sin. In his new book, "The Cross Worked.," Zach Maldonado helps these dear believers enter into the glory of their total forgiveness so they can experience the abundant life that Jesus offered to all who come to Him by faith. Devour this book and enter into the freedom of your birthright in Christ!

- Frank Friedmann, Teaching Pastor at Grace Life Fellowship

Zach Maldonado's book *The Cross Worked.* has earned a place on Scope Ministries International's recommended reading list as well as our training required reading list. Mr. Maldonado expertly uses Scripture to reveal common misunderstandings concerning the believer's walk with God. These misunderstandings affect our ability to walk with confidence in Him. I recommend this book whole-heartedly. A word of caution: Make sure you buy multiple copies to pass around to friends and family!

- Dr. Scott Hadden, President of Scope Ministries International

Your sins have been forgiven. The work has been done. Walk with Zach through the pages of this book, and let this amazing truth fill your heart with confidence and turn your guilt and fear into rest and peace.

- Bob Christopher, author of *Simple Gospel, Simply Grace* and radio host of Basic Gospel.

Zach has written a refreshingly CLEAR book on the goodness and finished work of Jesus! Zach encourages us to live, breathe and move "from grace, not for grace." This book is just what I have been looking for to share with others on how they can be confident in their relationship with God for today and in their last earthly breath. I'm not exaggerating - I LOVE THIS BOOK!!

- Tracy Levinson, bestselling author of *unashamed - candid conversations about dating, love, nakedness & faith*

In *The Cross Worked.*, Zach does an excellent job of walking through exactly what happens when we place our faith in Jesus and he does so with a deep grounding in the Bible. In this book, you'll find verse after verse and truth after truth to set you free from any misconception you may have about your new identity in Christ.

- Zach Lambert, Lead Pastor at Restore Austin

Zach's biblical knowledge of God's grace runs deep within these pages. His gift of communicating just how secure we are in Jesus Christ was astounding! If you are looking for a confidence-building book, backed up by tons of Scripture, this is the read for you!

- Matt McMillen, Author of *60 Days For Jesus*

Zach Maldonado truly stands out as one of those brilliant young Grace preachers of our time. He gets it! The cross was enough. Christ finished the work. God's grace is sufficient! Never before has the New Covenant message of total forgiveness and no condemnation been so needed, especially in a culture of youth who are constantly terrorized by the fear-based preaching and teaching so prevalent in the church. This book is clear and powerful proof that Zach knows his subject and is deeply qualified to teach it. You will get a greater grasp of God's grace as you read.

- **Tony Sutherland**, Speaker, Author, Worship Leader, Atlanta, GA

The Cross Worked. had me grinning from ear to ear with each page. It's a super-concentrated dose of "It is finished!" Zach does a fantastic job of explaining several passages that come up in every Q & A about the message of pure grace because of misinterpretations of certain scriptures that cause fear for believers. Zach applies the truth clearly and decisively. Finally we have a book that addresses a multitude of doubts and points the reader to the completed, final, eternal work of Jesus, bringing great peace to the conscience!

- **Tricia Gunn**, founder of Parresia and author of *Unveiling Jesus*

Zach comes out swinging in *The Cross Worked.*, and he doesn't pull any punches. If you're looking for nice little antidotes, poems and stories, go somewhere else. From the first page, Zach lays out a straightforward, no-nonsense explanation of the gospel of grace. Most people know that Jesus is significant, but they don't really know why. In *The Cross Worked.* you get a comprehensive and compelling explanation of why Jesus matters! I'm a grace preacher, and this book has already got me more fired up than I've ever been!

- Jason Mayfield, Pastor, Speaker, and President of Grace For Life

Zach Maldonado shares the truth of the Gospel of grace through the lens of his passion and experience for encouragement and practical application like no one else can. *The Cross Worked.* will help you know all Christ has done for you and all He is to and in you. Even more than that, Zach's zeal for you to rest in Christ's finished work will inspire you daily to know and enjoy Life with Jesus even more for yourself. Devour this book. You will forever enjoy God enjoying you by grace as a result!

- Mike Q. Daniel, International speaker and director at ZoeCode.org

Zach has written a clear and intriguing primer for God's amazing grace. This book is a sure-fire conversation starter.

- **Andrew Nelson**, author of *Children of the King* and *Fight for Grace*

If you're looking for some fresh and challenging insight to some old and traditional ways of thinking, this book is for you. Zach does a great job utilizing Scripture as the basis of his invitation to our freedom in Christ!

- **Steve Eden**, Lead Pastor of Grace Church

I believe Zach is a voice of grace to a new generation. I highly recommend his book *"The Cross Worked."* as a teaching tool and a study guide for those hungry for the truth about total and complete forgiveness. By the time you finish it you will be convinced of what JESUS did on your behalf and that because of it you are the righteousness of God. Sit back, grab a cup of coffee and prepare to be convinced because "The Cross Worked."

- **Wynema Clark**, New Covenant For Housewives

Zach has provided a clear concise pronouncement of our freedom in Christ. When so many are living under the burden of the old covenant, or saddled with treadmill Christianity, Zach shows that who Jesus has set free is free indeed.

- Jeff Harris, Senior Pastor of Grace Point Church

Zach is a great friend of mine, but an even better man of God. His heart for helping the most free people on earth: Christians, live freely, is shown throughout the pages of this book. *The Cross Worked.* pierces the shackles that have been put on the human heart by religion and frees us to walk in the confidence of the Cross. *The Cross Worked.* will help you see that Jesus is in love with you, right where you are.

- Benjamin Patrick, Pastor and Speaker

THE**CROSS**WORKED.

WHY YOU CAN HAVE
CONFIDENCE
ON THE DAY OF JUDGMENT

Zach Maldonado

THE CROSS WORKED.

©2018 by Zach Maldonado

Italics in Scripture quotations are the author's emphasis.

Unless otherwise indicated, Scripture quotations are from:

The Holy Bible, *English Standard Version* (ESV)

©2001 by Crossway Bibles, a division of Good News Publishers. Used by permission. All rights reserved.

Other Scripture quotations are from:

New American Standard Bible ® (NASB) ©1960, 1977, 1995 by the Lockman Foundation. Used by permission.

Copyright © 1995-2014 by ISV Foundation. ALL RIGHTS RESERVED INTERNATIONALLY. Used by permission of Davidson Press, LLC. The author has added italics to Scripture quotations for emphasis.

ISBN-13: 978-1984959355
ISBN-10: 1984959352

Contents

INTRODUCTION

If the truth you're hearing isn't setting you free, then it's not the truth.

I wasn't being set free by what I was hearing either. This is why I had to reexamine everything I believed. Once I got back to Scripture, I realized that the gospel is really good news, and that God really is good.

Perhaps you're living in constant fear of what God thinks about you. Maybe you don't have confidence in what He did for you and what He thinks of you. If you're tired of a god who only wants you to do more or be better, then this book is for you. If you're confused about the mixed messages you've been hearing, then this book is for you. And if you're burned out because you were told you have to do more for God, then this book is for you.

My heart in writing this book is to look at what the Bible says about the *forgiveness* of our sins, and how that changes the way we see God and the final judgment. More than likely, you've heard that God forgives you with some strings attached. Although many will say God's love is without condition, each Sunday, many of us hear only more conditions. We're told we have to do more, be better, or try harder.

After hearing this message, we eventually get worn out. But I'm here to tell you that the gospel is good news about a God who is good to you. And who has come to give you rest and confidence.

Jesus promised us rest for our souls, not more work. In this book, we'll discover that we can have rest because Jesus paid it all. He not only forgave us of all our sins, but He also freed us from any fear of judgment for those sins. When we look to the cross, we look at what Jesus did to freely give us rest, confidence, and relationship with God.

Although many of us have heard mixed messages in the name of God, we need to realize God is not a double-talker; nor is He a God of confusion. The double-talk we hear today means we need to reexamine some of our long-held beliefs about God and our relationship with Him.

As we journey through this book, we'll look to Scripture and see some amazing truths, such as:

- We're forgiven of all our sins—past, present, and future.

- God will not judge us for our sins.
- We are just like Jesus.
- We can have confidence, not fear, on the day of judgment.
- We cannot lose our salvation.

After reading this book, my hope and prayer is that you can believe the cross is enough, and realize that what Jesus did actually worked and that we're forever forgiven and secure because of Him. As we look to Scripture, we'll see that the truth always sets us free.

REASON 1

YOU'RE TOTALLY FORGIVEN

CHAPTER 1

Past, Present, and Future

You're forgiven of all sins! Yes, past, present, and future!

Tell this to some believers, and they think you're crazy. But a closer look at what Jesus did for us reveals that if our sins are not all forgiven, then we're without hope. The reason most of us don't believe we're totally forgiven is that we have a sin-by-sin system for forgiving sin. We forgive sin when it's committed or when someone asks us for forgiveness. However, God doesn't have a sin-by-sin system for forgiving sin.

Under the old covenant, Israel had a year-by-year forgiveness system for forgiving sin, which would happen on the Day of Atonement. In Catholicism, church members are required to seek forgiveness based on confession to a priest. And in most Protestant circles, forgiveness is based on confession of sin and asking for it.

However, the New Testament tells us that God does not forgive us sin by sin, confession by confession, or when we ask for it. Instead, Hebrews 9:22 says, *"Without the shedding of blood there is no forgiveness of sins."* God's system is blood. Not confession, not going to a priest, and not asking for it daily.

This means that blood and nothing else brings about forgiveness. Jesus shed His blood, and this brought forgiveness of sins. Since He shed His blood only once, and will never shed it again, our forgiveness is a done deal.

This is God's process of forgiving sins. It's like the system in our world where, in order to get something, we must pay for it. If I want gasoline, then I must pay for it first in order to receive it. In the same way, in order to have our sins forgiven, blood must be shed as the payment for our forgiveness so that we can receive it. This is God's way.

God forgives only with the shedding of blood—nothing else. Jesus shed His blood only once, and He will never shed it again. Therefore God forgives sins one time for all time. Hebrews calls this forgiveness "once for all."

This once-for-all forgiveness means that Jesus offered Himself one time for all sins. Hebrews 7:27 puts it this way:

> He has no need, like those high priests, to offer sacrifices daily, first for his own sins and then for those of the people, since he did this once for all when he offered up himself.

Since Jesus is not shedding His blood daily, we're not being forgiven day by day. Jesus, unlike the priests of the Old Testament, does not need to offer Himself repeatedly (Hebrews 9:25) because He has "appeared once for all at the end of the ages to put away sin by the sacrifice of himself" (Hebrews 9:26).

This means that Jesus does not have to die and shed His blood again, because His shed blood was sufficient for *all* sins—past, present, and future. When we sin, Jesus doesn't have to come down and shed His blood again because His blood removed all of our sins the first time. If Jesus had to shed His blood again, this would mean His first offering was not sufficient. But we know that what Jesus did worked the first time.

Put another way, since only blood effects forgiveness, and Jesus shed His blood only once and will not shed it again, believers are forgiven once for all.

As a result of Christ's one offering, Hebrews 10 says that we are "made holy" once for all (10:10), and "perfected for all time" (10:14). In the Old Testament, believers could never be made perfect or cleansed (Hebrews 10:1-2), but through Jesus, we've been perfectly cleansed and forgiven forever. Further, we've been set apart—sanctified—once and for all. The reason we can be set apart once and for all is that what Jesus did for us (and to us) worked!

Additionally, we see that God chooses to remember our sins no more: "I will remember their sins and their lawless deeds no more" (Hebrews 10:17). The only reason He can do this is that what Jesus did on our behalf was enough to take away all our sins. God promises right now that He will not hold our sins against us for any reason. This is why, when Christ returns, He does not have to deal with our sins again:

> So Christ, having been offered once to bear the sins of many, will appear a second time, not to deal with sin but to save those who are eagerly waiting for him. (Hebrews 9:28)

Maybe you're thinking, *How can God forgive future sins?* There are a few reasons for this. First, how many of your sins were in the future when Christ shed His blood? All of them. Second, God is not bound by time, and has seen your entire life and chosen to forgive and forget every one of your sins.

Still have doubts? Read this slowly: "By one offering He has perfected *for all time* those who are sanctified" (Hebrews 10:14 NASB).

Hebrews 10:18 solidifies the writer's argument for

once-for-all forgiveness by saying, "Where there *is forgiveness* of these, there is *no longer* any offering for sin." Put simply, since all sins have been taken away once for all, there's no need for any more offerings, because Jesus's one offering *worked!*

It is *done*. If you've placed your faith in Jesus Christ, you're a forgiven person.

This is why Jesus is seated at the right hand of God. His work for our forgiveness is done. Hebrews 10:11-12 reveals the difference between the old covenant priests and Jesus:

> And every priest stands daily at his service, offering repeatedly the same sacrifices, which can never take away sins. But when Christ had offered for all time a single sacrifice for sins, he sat down at the right hand of God.

In the Old Testament, believers had to constantly have their sins atoned for. And this atonement could never remove or forgive sins. But in the New Testament, Christians are not having to be continuously forgiven or cleansed. We are totally forgiven forever. And completely cleansed, once and for all.

Jesus is seated because He no longer needs to do something in order for us to be forgiven. The priests of the old covenant could never sit down because their work was never done. Their sacrifices had to always be repeated. In contrast, Jesus's one sacrifice needs no repeat because it worked the first time and for all time.

For this reason, Jesus shouted *"It is finished"* on the cross. Jesus does not have to come down to shed His blood or to offer Himself again because His one offering has perfectly forgiven us forever. He is not shedding His blood continuously, and we're not being forgiven continuously. In regard to our forgiveness, the work is done. Jesus has closed shop. And He's now resting at the right hand of God!

Therefore, because of what Jesus has done, believers now have *"confidence* to enter the holy places by the blood of Jesus" (Hebrews 10:19). Under the old covenant, only the high priest could enter God's presence at a set time. But now, through our total forgiveness, believers can enter God's presence freely and confidently.

In Hebrews 4:16, this entry and confidence are spoken of again: "Let us then with *confidence* draw near to the throne of grace." The only reason we can have confidence to enter God's presence is that we're forgiven and cleansed. To say that the Holy God would allow unforgiven and imperfectly cleansed people into His presence is to denigrate God's holiness.

God is perfectly holy and thus makes us perfectly holy

in order for us to be in His presence. This is why the New Testament tells us again and again that we are *saints*—holy, sanctified, and righteous.[1]

In summary:

- Only blood achieves forgiveness (Hebrews 9:22; 10:10, 14).
- Jesus shed His blood and will not shed it again (Hebrews 7:27; 9:25-28).
- Believers are forgiven once for all through Christ's single offering (Hebrews 10:10-14).
- This means that no further offering for sin is needed, since all sins—past, present, and future—have been forgiven once and for all (Hebrews 10:18).
- Therefore, we can have confidence to go to God, since all our sins are forgiven.

Defined by Jesus

Are you haunted by your past mistakes? Since we're forgiven of all our sins, we're free to fix our eyes on Jesus, not on our past. Our total forgiveness means we're no longer defined by what we've done. We're defined by what Jesus has done for us. Instead of worrying about what we did, we can trust in what Jesus has already done. We can relax in knowing our sins are all gone.

Maybe you're still facing the consequences of past sins. The truth is still the same. Those sins and their consequences don't define you. When you came to Jesus, He gave you a new future and a new past. He tore up your past record, and He gave you His perfect record. And now, He's not keeping score.

God is not holding your past, present, or future sins against you. God has redeemed it all and is working it all for your good. Your past may make you feel dirty, but Jesus has made you clean. Your past may make you feel distant from God, but Jesus has made you close. Through Jesus, you are clean, close to Him, and totally forgiven.

We can have confidence, not fear, before God. Why? He has taken away our sins. He has cleansed us. And He calls us His beloved children. When you sin, God is not shaking His head in disappointment. Instead, He is reminding you the cross is enough. You are forgiven. You are cleansed. And you are deeply loved.

Total forgiveness means that even at your absolute worst, God's love for you will not change. We can be confident in God's forgiveness of our sins, because it's not about us and what we do. It's about Jesus and what He did.

CHAPTER 2

Nothing Left to Forgive

Our confidence doesn't rest in what we do for God, but in what Jesus has done for us. It's His shed blood that brings forgiveness. And His sacrifice for us is the proof by which we know we're totally forgiven. The New Testament shouts to us that we're completely forgiven and that this forgiveness is solely tied to Jesus and His shed blood.

Blood in the New Testament

Blood as the only way by which God forgives is a theme echoed throughout the New Testament. By His blood we are declared right (justified): "We have now been justified by his blood" (Romans 5:9), and therefore we have perfect peace with God (5:1). Why is this? Because Jesus took away our sin.

Let's think about it. What's the one thing that caused us to be enemies of God? *Sin*. What did Jesus do with our sin? *He took it all away.*

As a result, we now have peace with God because of the take-away and complete forgiveness of our sins. In Romans 5:1, peace with God is a stated fact, something that cannot be changed. Peace with God is the present reality we get to enjoy, not something we hope for when we hit heaven.

Paul goes on to say that we are reconciled (our relationship with God restored) by the death of Christ (Romans 5:10). We've been both restored and made right. Notice that both these things are accomplished through the death and shed blood of Jesus. We're brought into right relationship with God only because Jesus has taken away our sins forever. And by taking away our sins, He has also taken away any punishment for those sins.

If Jesus didn't take away our sins forever, then our relationship with God would be no different from that of people in the old covenant. But what sets the new covenant apart is that Jesus has done what the law could never do: remove sins and bring us into right relationship with God forever.

The New Testament goes on to say that we are ransomed by Christ's blood (1 Peter 1:18-19; Revelation 5:9). We are cleansed from all sin by His blood (1 John 1:8). We are freed from our sins by His blood (Revelation 1:5). We are redeemed and forgiven through His blood (Ephesians 1:7). And we are brought near to God by Christ's blood (Ephesians 2:13).

It is blood and nothing else that brings about the forgiveness, closeness, and cleansing we need. If these things could come any other way, then Christ died in vain. But He did not die in vain, which is why believers are cleansed from their sin, forgiven of their sin, and brought close to their heavenly Father.

Forgiveness in the New Testament

Apart from a few verses that we'll address soon, the New Testament is clear that forgiveness is a completed work. As you'll see, all these references speak of our forgiveness in the past tense, as a finished work.

Our redemption and forgiveness is a completed work. If we believe in Jesus, then we're forgiven and redeemed. We're not waiting or hoping for forgiveness from God; we *have* it. To be redeemed means to be forgiven. You cannot have one without the other.

> We have redemption, the forgiveness of sins. (Colossians 1:14)

> In him we have redemption through his blood, the forgiveness of our trespasses. (Ephesians 1:7)

Combining the truth of Colossians 2:13 ("God made us alive together with him, having forgiven us all our trespasses") with the truth of 1 John 2:12 ("Your sins are forgiven for his name's sake"), we realize the message is clear: we're forgiven people. The work is done. We don't have to beg or plead or wait for God to forgive us. Our sins are forgiven.

Our total forgiveness is why we can forgive other people. Our forgiveness of others' offenses toward us is rooted in God's forgiveness of our own sins. Colossians 3:13 says we ought to be "forgiving each other; as the Lord has forgiven you." And Ephesians 4:32 says that we're to be "forgiving one another, as God in Christ forgave you."

We forgive because we've been forgiven. If our forgiveness wasn't total or complete, then we would have to wait for God to forgive us in order to forgive others. But that's not the message. We're forgiven so that we can forgive.

All these verses are blanket statements. That's why Paul in Romans 6 had to address people who might want to take advantage of this scandalous grace. If our forgiveness was conditioned upon our repeated asking and confessing, then people would never think they could abuse God's grace.

However, since our forgiveness is total and complete, we have Romans 6. In this chapter, Paul says the believer is "united with Christ" (6:5), "set free from sin" (6:7), "dead to sin and alive to God" (6:11), an "instrument of righteousness" (6:12), and "obedient from the heart" (6:17). This shatters the idea that "too much grace" or total forgiveness is a "license to sin."

God was not naïve when He decided to forgive all our sins. He also made us new. For this reason, total forgiveness makes sense, because it's accompanied by our being made brand new.

Our motivation to avoid sin does not arise from an intention to get more forgiveness from God. Our motivation to avoid sin is rooted in the new identity God has given us. We cannot out-sin God's grace (Roman 5:20)—but by His grace, we no longer want to.

We don't want to sin since we're now slaves of righteousness (Romans 6:18). Yes, we all stumble in many ways (James 3:2), but as children of God we now want what God wants. The apostle Paul gives us plenty of reasons to avoid sin and not abuse grace, but getting additional forgiveness from God wasn't one of them.

The Unforgivable Sin

The New Testament speaks of a sin that's unforgivable—blasphemy of the Holy Spirit (Mark 3:29). This is simply the lifelong rejection of Jesus Christ as Lord and Savior. This sin is described as eternal because when someone commits it, he or she is actively choosing to reject Jesus. Jesus cannot forgive and save someone who doesn't want to be saved or forgiven.

The good news for the believer is that we cannot commit blasphemy of the Holy Spirit, because we've called upon the name of Jesus and we want Him to save us. Even "if we are faithless, he remains faithful" (2 Timothy 2:13).

If God forgave the whole world of all sins, then there would be no need for faith or repentance. Since the entire world is not saved, forgiveness and salvation is found only in Christ, through faith. This is why there's still one sin that separates one from God: blasphemy of the Holy Spirit. Every unbeliever is committing this sin, and God is actively pursuing them in the hope that they will believe in Him. God wants none to perish but for all to turn to Him (2 Peter 3:9).

It's worth noting also that the unforgivable sin is not suicide, nor is suicide "the sin that leads to death" mentioned in 1 John 5. The sin leading to death is the unrepentant rejection of the gospel and of Jesus Christ as Lord and Savior (1 John 5:16); in fact, the entire letter of 1 John is dedicated to contrasting those who are saved with those who are not.

To say that God sends to hell a believer who makes a bad choice to kill himself totally misses the heart of God. Nowhere in Scripture does it say that suicide is the unforgivable sin or that it's different from any other sin. Our forgiveness is not rooted in how little or small our sins are. Our forgiveness is based on the shed blood of Jesus. There's no such thing as big sins and small sins—there are only sins. And Jesus took them all away.

How to Receive It

Total, once-for-all forgiveness is found only in Jesus Christ. In order to receive this amazing forgiveness of all your sins—past, present, and future—you simply have to "confess with your mouth that Jesus is Lord and believe in your heart that God raised him from the dead, and you will be saved" (Romans 10:9).

That's it. It's that simple. We're saved by grace through faith, not by works. Why? "So that no one may boast" (Ephesians 2:9). The apostle Paul said it best: "May it never be that I would boast, except in the cross of our Lord Jesus Christ" (Galatians 6:14 NASB).

Are you willing to place all your hope and trust in Jesus Christ? And are you willing to believe that everything He did for you through the cross and resurrection *worked*? If so, pray this prayer with me:

> Jesus, I believe that You are Lord. I believe that God raised You from the dead. And right now, I trust You as my Savior and my life. Thank You for forgiving me of all of my sins. Thank You for giving me a new identity in you. Thank You for coming to live inside me. And thank You for freeing me from my sin. In this moment, I believe that the cross worked, and that You, Jesus Christ, are enough. Amen.

CHAPTER 3

1 John 1:9

Perhaps the single most misunderstood verse in the New Testament is 1 John 1:9. This verse has caused centuries of believers to doubt whether they were really forgiven. Even though there are dozens of verses that speak of our total forgiveness in Christ, this one "proof text" has confused many of us. And I believe once we look at the context of this verse, we'll discover that the truth always sets us free.

The common understanding of 1 John 1:9 is that we confess our sins in order to receive forgiveness from God. Within this statement lies a few problems. The first problem is a contradiction in Scripture. If only blood brings forgiveness, how can confession over the life of a believer bring forgiveness? Further, if confession of every sin can bring forgiveness, then why did Jesus have to shed His blood?

The other problem is the impossibility of confessing every sin. We sin a lot over the period of our life, and do we really remember to confess each one? Not only that, but

John relates confession of sin to fellowship, which to John is equivalent to salvation.[2] Does this mean believers have to confess each sin in order to stay in fellowship with God and to stay saved? This would create another problem— salvation by works.

As we'll see, 1 John 1:9 is a verse directed to unbelievers in hopes they will recognize their need for Jesus.[3]

The Audience

1 John 1 is dealing with people who don't have fellowship with God (1:3), and John's goal is for them to have that fellowship. For John, to have fellowship with God is to be saved; to not have fellowship means you are not saved. These people are therefore not saved and not true believers. Scholars suggest they were either secessionists—those who thought they were sinless [4] —or they believed in Docetism, which are those who reject the incarnate Son of God.[5]

Not every verse in the Bible is written to believers. There were both believers and unbelievers in every church, which is why context is crucial in understanding Scripture.

Throughout John's writings, and the New Testament, light and darkness are two opposing metaphors. They are used as good and evil; life and death; God's kingdom and Satan's kingdom; and the place of the believer and non-believer.[6] People in the New Testament are either in the light and saved, or in the darkness and not saved.

As we look through 1 John, it's crucial to understand that John uses "us" and "we" as a rhetorical device in order to communicate that if any of his readers fulfill these descriptions, they're in need of confession.

The conditions found in verses 6, 8, and 10, are in direct contrast to what the rest of John reveals about believers. For example, John says, believers are forgiven (2:12), have the word in them (2:14), and know the truth (2:21). This is in contrast to the audience in 1 John 1 who walk in darkness (1:6), do not practice the truth (1:6), do not have truth in them (1:8), and do not have the word in them (1:10). The audience of 1 John chapter 1 is clearly not believers.

Bar of Soap?

Now that we know 1 John 1 is not about believers and their need to get more forgiveness. We can clearly see that 1 John 1:9 is not meant to be used as a "bar of soap" for daily cleansing for the believer. Instead, context will reveal that 1 John 1:9 is an invitation for unbelievers to believe in the gospel.

> This is the message we have heard from him and proclaim to you, that God is light, and in him is no darkness at all. If we say we have fellowship with him while we walk in darkness, we lie and do not practice the truth. (1 John 1:5-6)

John proclaims to them here that God is light and in Him there is no darkness, which is the theme John will unpack in verses 6-10. The term "those who walk in darkness" (1:6) does not refer to believers who sin, because we all stumble in many ways (James 3:2), but to those who reject the truth, and reject their need for God.

> But if we walk in the light, as he is in the light, we have fellowship with one another, and the blood of Jesus his Son cleanses us from all sin. If we say we have no sin, we deceive ourselves, and the truth is not in us. If we confess our sins, he is faithful and just to forgive us our sins and to cleanse us from all unrighteousness. If we say we have not sinned, we make him a liar, and his word is not in us. (1 John 1:7-10)

In contrast to verse 6, those who walk in the light (1:7), are those who accept Jesus, and recognize their need for God. Although those who walk in the light may sin, they've already been cleansed by Jesus's blood from all sin (1:7).

Verses 6 and 7 have the same structure as verses 8 and 9. They contrast each other to show the difference between an unbeliever and how to be a believer. These verses are not contrasting two different believers.

Those who walk in darkness say they have no sin (1:8) and that they have not sinned (1:10), which implies their rejection of God—blasphemy—the only sin that cannot be forgiven. John affirms that these people are not believers by saying the truth is not in them (1:8). For this reason, John says they need to confess their sins so that God can forgive them of all unrighteousness. Therefore, 1 John 1:9 is a verse meant to lead those who say they do not have sin (v. 8) or have not sinned (v. 10) to acknowledge their sin in order to be saved.

To be clear, confession doesn't mean the verbal listing of every sin, but an acknowledgment that one has sinned.[7] God promises to both forgive and cleanse, which, these verbs, "being aorist subjunctive in form, portray forgiveness and purification as complete, rather than ongoing actions."[8] And that's why 1 John 1:9 says *all* unrighteousness, not just some.

John goes on to reveal that 1 John 1:9 was written to unbelievers, by opening up chapter 2 addressing his audience—believers—as "my little children." And he says that if they sin, they have an advocate (1 John 2:1).

Now, if confession of sins for forgiveness was God's way of forgiving the believer, why wouldn't John say, "if we sin, we can confess and be forgiven"? He does not say this because 1 John 1:9 is not for believers. Believers are forgiven people.

That's why John goes on to say, "I am writing to you, little children, because your sins are forgiven for his name's sake" (1 John 2:12). For John, the believer's forgiveness is not in doubt. It's a done deal. Believers *are* forgiven.

This is why 1 John 1:9 isn't meant to be used for daily cleansing for the believer. Nowhere in John's writings or the rest of the New Testament is confession used as a prayer to God, but as a public acknowledgment.[9] John is trying to get these people in the church to openly confess their need for Jesus so that they can have fellowship with them.

Some argue that since the verb *confess* in the original language is in the active tense, it means believers must continue to confess their sins. But it's clear that verse 9 isn't speaking to believers, but to those who fit the condition of verse 8 and verse 10. Verse 9 is saying that whenever you (the sin denier) want to confess, you can, and God will forgive you.

Further, the reason the verb *confess* is in the present tense is that the phrase "if we" is in question. John is unsure if they'll confess, but he's saying the offer is always on the table.

Compare this with verses 6 and 7. If we were to go by the traditional teaching that verse 9 is meant for believers as ongoing confession and applied that same logic to verse 7, then is the believers' cleansing and fellowship based on their ability to walk in the light like verse 7 says? Absolutely not! This would be another form of works-based righteousness.

If we could be cleansed and brought into fellowship with God by what we do, then Christ died in vain. The cross would be pointless. Instead, John is comparing verses 6 and 7 by saying that if you believe in Jesus, are a child of the light, and thus walk in the light, then you're cleansed and do not walk in darkness. In the same way, if you've confessed your sin, then you're forgiven and cleansed of all unrighteousness.

In summary, 1 John 1:9 is about acknowledging that one has sinned, needs a savior, and through faith in Christ can receive forgiveness. It's not our confession of every sin that brings forgiveness. It's the blood of Christ that brings forgiveness. It's not our confession of every sin that brings us into fellowship with God, but our one-time confession that we've sinned and need God.

Some may object and say this verse means that we need to confess only the big sins or the ones we remember. But there's no blood being shed when believers confess their sins to God, therefore there's no forgiveness happening. Furthermore, is our theology "God forgives the sins that we forget," and that He automatically forgives the "little sins" but we need to make sure we fess up to the "big ones?" Let's respect the work of Christ and trust that it was enough. If believers need more forgiveness from God, then the cross did not work.

Everyone agrees that at salvation, all sins to that point have been forgiven. But the problem is those same people say after salvation, it's up to us to maintain our forgiveness. In other words, not only does the system for forgiveness change, but according to them, the gospel gets worse!

However, the gospel is good news for every single day. And the gospel is that Jesus has forgiven us of all our sins, forever.

There's only one system for being forgiven—blood. It's Jesus's shed blood and work that I'm trusting in, not my memory, confession, or work.

Let's trust that the cross actually worked!

The Role of Confession

If believers don't need to confess their sins in order to be forgiven, then what's the role of confession for the believer? As we look at the rest of Scripture, we see that confession of sins to God is healthy. Talk to Dad. Be open and honest with Him about your struggles.

I've found that sharing my struggles with God allows me to remember my once-for-all forgiveness and cleansing. I can talk to Him with confidence knowing that He has forgiven and forgotten my sins. We don't have to hide from Him or be scared. He loves us. He is crazy about us. And He knows how to help us in our weakness with His all sufficient, comforting grace. We can run to God with confidence because the cross worked.

We need not have the fear of accidentally missing a confessed sin. We have the choice to confess. God just wants to talk to us, to help us, and to comfort us in our time of weakness. God has seen all of our sins and has forgiven them. God is not asking us to keep up with our sins. He is asking us trust in His sacrifice.

Additionally, confession to one another is healthy for the believer. James 5:16 tells us to "confess your sins to one another and pray for one another, that you may be healed." Find trusted friends that you can share your sins and struggles with. There's freedom in being able to share your sins with other believers who love you.

The freedom in sharing your sins with others comes from the fact that they're able to remind you that your sins are forgiven and forgotten. In sharing, you rip off the mask that shame and guilt have given you, and you allow yourself to be loved. You allow yourself to soak in the total forgiveness Jesus has given you.

CHAPTER 4

Fellowship with God

Some say that we need to confess our sins or ask for forgiveness in order to stay in fellowship with God. But the false idea that Christians can lose fellowship with God is based on a low view of God's punishment. The wages of sin is death (Romans 6:23), not a lesser punishment—like loss of fellowship.

We can be confident that God is not punishing Christians any longer because all the punishment for our sin was taken by Christ on the cross (Romans 8:3). The wages of sin is death, and Jesus died and took our punishment so we wouldn't have to. That's why "there is therefore now no condemnation for those who are in Christ Jesus" (Romans 8:1).

This "no condemnation" isn't based on how well the believer lives, but on the total forgiveness of the believer based on the work of Christ. Put another way, we are free from condemnation because of Jesus, not because of how we perform. And since we're free from condemnation, we're free from punishment. which means God is not going to punish us by leaving us.

Connected Forever

Our connection with Christ is never lost. Christ is within us, every moment of every day. This is why we cannot lose fellowship with God. Our fellowship is permanent. God will never leave us.

Hebrews 13:5 reads, "For He Himself has said, 'I will never desert you, nor will I ever forsake you.'" How we understand fellowship with God must be based on the fact that God will never leave us for any reason.

Those who say we can lose fellowship with God say sin is the reason. But what did God do with our sin? He took it away, forever. Therefore, God will never leave us or forsake us.

Another crucial verse for understanding our connection with God is 1 Corinthians 6:17 (NASB): "But the one who joins himself to the Lord is one spirit with Him." We are one with Christ. Can we get any closer than that? God cannot distance Himself from us because He has chosen to unite Himself with us.

It's also worth noting that there's no verse in the New

Testament that speaks of believers going in and out of fellowship with God. The New Testament simply says we have fellowship or do not have fellowship. It's black or white. Either you are saved and have fellowship with God, or are lost and do not have fellowship with God.

You Cannot Lose It

Fellowship with God is talked about most in 1 John 1. In this chapter, we see that you're either saved and in fellowship or lost and out of fellowship. In 1 John 1:3, John reveals the purpose of his writing and the fact that he has fellowship with the Father and the Son.

John's purpose in writing this letter was for his audience to enjoy the same fellowship with the church and with God that he and the apostles enjoyed. To John, fellowship with believers also means fellowship with God.

John then reveals that those who walk in darkness are liars and do not have fellowship with God (1:6). He contrasts this in verse 7 by saying if we walk in the light, then we have fellowship with one another. It's crucial to see here that fellowship isn't talked about as an "in and out" concept. Rather, fellowship is related to our union with Christ that's possible only through salvation. Put simply, if you're saved, you have fellowship with God.

Although Christians who walk in the light do sin, this does not prevent our fellowship with God because He has removed our sin as far as the east is from the west (Psalm 103:12). And He chooses to not hold our sin against us (Hebrews 10:17).

John reveals in verse 7 that the conditions necessary for fellowship with God is fulfilled by the death of Jesus Christ. We have fellowship with one another (which means we have fellowship with God) only because we're cleansed from all sin. Our fellowship is both initiated by Christ and sustained by Him. He brought us into fellowship with God through His blood. And He will keep us in fellowship with God.

Think about it. What's the one thing that caused us to lose relationship and fellowship with God? *Sin*. What did Jesus do with our sin? *He took it away forever*. Consequently, we can enjoy fellowship with God forever. The take-away of our sins means we're in fellowship with God forever.

God promises us that "nothing can snatch us from his hand" (John 10:29), and that we are "seated with Christ" (Ephesians 2:6) in heaven, making us as connected to God as we'll ever be.

Paul goes even further to say that we've been "brought near by the blood of Christ" (Ephesians 2:13), not by our behavior or performance. God has "called us into the fellowship of his Son" (1 Corinthians 1:9), and He is faithful to keep us to the end (Philippians 1:6; Jude 24).

This means that when we sin, God goes with us. This is why sin is no longer fun for the believer. We have died to sin and become slaves of righteousness (Romans 6:11). If we lost fellowship with God every time we sinned, then how could God promise us that He would never leave us or forsake us?

Jesus became our sin so that we could become His righteousness and never lose fellowship with God. Christians cannot lose fellowship with God because our sins have been taken away, our punishment for our sins have been poured out on Jesus, and God promises to never leave us. Even "when we are faithless, he remains faithful" (2 Timothy 2:13).

In regard to our fellowship with God, the cross worked.

The Cure for Loneliness

We all feel lonely. If you're like me, I feel loneliest after I sin, or after a rough day at work. Whatever the situation, we've all felt lonely and will all feel lonely.

We often base truth on how we feel. But just because we feel or don't feel something doesn't determine whether it's true. I know that gravity is keeping my feet on the ground, but I don't know if I feel that or think about it, do you? Do you feel the earth spinning? I don't. But I know it's true.

God can never leave us. He cannot lie. And since He cannot lie, He will not leave us, no matter what. This is good news. No matter how lonely we feel, God is always with us. No matter how dark our circumstances get, God is still within us.

It's not about feeling the presence of God within you. It's about knowing that no matter what you feel, God is fully present—all the time.

We can be confident that God is with us because He has taken away our sins, forever. You are safe in the Father's hand. You're united with Christ. And the Holy Spirit is living within you. The entire Trinity is with you, no matter what.

God has cleared out His entire schedule just to be with you. You don't have to feel the pressure of "making time for God." He has made time for you, and He will be with you all day.

You are never, ever alone.

CHAPTER 5

The Lord's Prayer

The New Testament does not begin in Matthew 1. Sure, when you open up your Bible to Matthew, one page before reads: "The New Testament." But *testament* can also mean covenant, and in order for a covenant to start, there must be a death. That's why the New Testament did not start at the birth of Jesus, but at the death of Jesus.

For this reason, Hebrews 9:15 says, the new covenant did not begin until Jesus's death. And Paul says Jesus was born under the law (old covenant) in order to redeem those under the law (Galatians 4:4).

I say all this to provide context to the Lord's Prayer.[10] Jesus was born under the law and ministered to those who were living under the law. The new covenant hadn't started. Therefore, God's new way of forgiveness hadn't started because Jesus had not shed His blood. That's why you'll find no verse from Acts to Revelation about the need to ask God for forgiveness.

Once we place things in their proper context, we'll see once again that the truth in regard to the Lord's Prayer and our once-for-all forgiveness always sets us free.

Conditional Forgiveness?

In the Lord's Prayer in both Matthew and Luke's account, we see the need to ask God to "forgive us our debts, as we also have forgiven our debtors." Jesus then clarifies what He means:

> For if you forgive others their trespasses, your heavenly Father will also forgive you, but if you do not forgive others their trespasses, neither will your Father forgive your trespasses. (Matthew 6:14-15)

Mark 11:25 echoes this statement: "And whenever you stand praying, forgive, if you have anything against anyone, so that your Father also who is in heaven may forgive you your trespasses."

It's clear: forgiveness according to Jesus is conditional. This means that our forgiveness from God is based on our forgiveness of others.

This begs the question: If our forgiveness is conditional, then what was the point of the cross? Why do we need the cross if we can get our forgiveness through what we do?

If we're all honest, this conditional forgiveness buries us.

There's no way anyone can live up to this standard. This is why context is our friend. Jesus is ministering to those who are under the law and not under the new covenant of grace. This is before Jesus shed His blood, and the law was still in effect. The new covenant didn't go into effect until Christ's death.

In Matthew 5 and 6, Jesus is speaking to those who are under the law, and He's revealing the true standard of the law. This is why He says in Matthew 5:22-23:

> If you are offering your gift at the altar and there remember that your brother has something against you, leave your gift there before the altar and go. First be reconciled to your brother, and then come and offer your gift. (Matthew 5:22-23)

This passage was spoken when there was still an altar and a temple to go to. But there are no longer any altars or temples because there's no need for them. Jesus has taken away our sins. And we are now the temple of God (1 Corinthians 6:19).

If Jesus were ministering to us, then how could we go to the altar? We would all fail, since there are no more altars. All throughout the Sermon on the Mount, Jesus is elevating the law to reveal that no one can be saved through keeping the law. This is why Jesus came to fulfill the law since we could not.

We have a choice: we can choose to see the Lord's Prayer as a pre-cross prayer spoken to those under the law, or as conditional forgiveness binding to us today. The problem with the latter view is that it contradicts Hebrews 9:22 and 1 John 1:9. To hold this view would also mean you would have to be okay with the Scripture contradicting itself. Not only that, but to hold this view is the same as looking at Jesus's work on the cross and saying it's not needed.

Not only does the Lord's Prayer contradict God's blood system, but it also contradicts what the apostle Paul said. In Ephesians 4:32, Paul says, "Be kind to one another, tenderhearted, forgiving one another, as God in Christ forgave you." Notice the order, we forgive because God has already forgiven us.

Paul also says this same thing in Colossians 3:13. He says, "forgiving each other; as the Lord has forgiven you." This is in direct contradiction to the Lord's Prayer. The only way to solve this is by rightly dividing the word of God. Doing this, we see that Jesus was speaking under the law, and Paul is speaking under the new covenant. Under the new covenant, we forgive because we've been forgiven.

There's no mention of asking God for forgiveness from Acts to Revelation. Why is that? Because the writers understood that the cross was the dividing line between the old and new covenant. If asking God for forgiveness was for believers, wouldn't it be mentioned even once from Acts to Revelation? As we saw earlier, forgiveness from Acts to Revelation is always spoken of as a finished work.

As a side note, this isn't to say that everything Jesus said is not applicable to those of us living under the new covenant. But we must understand that He came to fulfill the law and to reveal the true standard of the law so that people under the law could see their need for Him.

In summary, we don't need to ask God to forgive us each time we sin. We're forgiven. And there's nothing left for us to do to get more forgiveness from God.

A New Way to Pray

When you pray, you aren't sending off prayers to a God who's far off, but a God who's closer than your skin. You aren't making a long distance phone call. You're talking in person with the One who loves you the most—your heavenly Father.

When you pray, God hears you. He is focused on you and listening to every word. There's no such thing as a "right way to pray." He loves every prayer. He loves hearing from you. No longer do you need to feel the need to beg or plead for God to forgive you. Perhaps a new way to pray is this: "Thank you, Father, for what you have done."

We don't need to spend our time over analyzing our mistakes, or thinking that God is mad at us for them. Our total forgiveness means that God is no longer mad at us. His goal is to show us each day that what He did was enough. We are safe. We are forgiven. And we are deeply loved.

We can be confident God hears us because He has taken away our sins with no strings attached.

CHAPTER 6

Two Kinds of Forgiveness?

Some popular teachers who cannot fathom our total forgiveness say that there are two kinds of forgiveness— forensic and parental. Now, as a side note, these terms do not appear in Scripture.

These teachers say that God has forgiven us of all our sins—past, present, and future—*forensically*, meaning, in God's eyes only. They say we also need ongoing "parental" forgiveness from God in order to remain in fellowship and to get continual cleansing from Him.

So not only are they saying that God has two systems for forgiveness, they're also saying He has two views of us—a heavenly view and an earthly view. Confused? So am I.

In regard to the Lord's Prayer, many of these teachers say that this forgiveness refers to the "parental" forgiveness of God. The problem with this view is, it completely minimizes the words of Jesus. Jesus didn't say this was "parental forgiveness" but clearly said that God would not forgive. He was serious. And I am going to take Him at His word and not minimize His words in order to fit a view.

Scholars call this type of interpretation "eisegesis," which is basically imposing one's interpretation onto the text. Instead of rightly dividing the word of God, these teachers are having to come up with words in order to understand the Lord's Prayer, since they cannot fathom that God would actually forgive us of all our sins through His shed blood. It's obvious that these teachers are imposing their ideas on the Lord's Prayer by coming up with the words "parental" and "forensic" to describe forgiveness.

Washing Feet for Forgiveness?

These teachers also use the example of Jesus washing His disciple's feet in John 13 as a way to explain these two types of forgiveness. They quote John 13:10:

> The one who has bathed does not need to wash, except for his feet, but is completely clean. And you are clean.

They say that bathing refers to our "forensic" forgiveness and washing of the feet refers to our "parental" forgiveness. But do you see two types of forgiveness in this passage? Do you see the word "parental" or "forensic"? It's not there.

Most modern scholars omit the phrase "except for his feet" because it's clear that Jesus's washing of the feet was a symbol of His total cleansing, not an additional cleansing we need.[11] They also omit this phrase because it's not seen in many early manuscripts, and scholars believe it was added later.

Further, it's true that in some regard Jesus is symbolizing His cleansing of us. He says in verse 8 that "If I do not wash you, you have no share with me." But notice that Jesus does not wash them again and again, but only once.

Jesus then offers the core interpretation of this passage and why He washed the disciple's feet:

> If I then, your Lord and Teacher, have washed your feet, you also ought to wash one another's feet. For I have given you an example, that you also should do just as I have done to you. (13:14-15)

Jesus was modeling to them the type of servanthood He desires from His followers. There's no mention in this passage of two types of forgiveness or an additional cleansing we need. There's no mention of forgiveness or anything to do with parental or forensic forgiveness. Jesus washed their feet as an example of servanthood, not as an analogy for forgiveness.

Once again, we see these teachers have imposed their ideas into the text in order to back up their interpretation. They're literally pulling terms and ideas out of thin air because they cannot believe that the cross actually worked!

They also use the analogy that our relationship with God is like our relationship with our kids. They will say, "Sure, God loves us and accepts us, but He has to forgive us each time we do or say something wrong, like we do with our kids."

The problem with this logic is that we don't have a blood system for forgiveness. And we did not shed our blood for our kids! Our relationship with God is better than any relationship we have on earth because it's all about Him!

This is why the rest of the New Testament says we were washed (1 Corinthians 6:11), and cleansed from our sins (2 Peter 1:9). This is also why the writer of Hebrews can confidently say we are perfected for all time (Hebrews 10:14).

We don't need any more cleansing or forgiveness. And there aren't two types of forgiveness or cleansing. What Jesus did for us and to us was real, not "forensic" or "parental." Through His real shed blood, we get to enjoy real forgiveness, right here and right now.

Enjoy Your Forgiveness

How can we enjoy our forgiveness? One way we do this is by trusting in what Jesus says about us, not what shame says. Shame says our sin has made us wrong, but Jesus says He has made us right. Shame says that our sin has made us dirty, but Jesus says, His sacrifice has made us clean.

When shame comes, and it will, we can choose to set our minds on what Jesus has done, not on what we just did. Jesus has taken our shame, so that we could take His acceptance. He took everything we did wrong so that we could forever be right.

In those moments when you feel most ashamed, God is shouting from your heart, "I am not ashamed to call you my child!" God isn't disappointed with you. He is not shaking His head at you. He loves you. And He will never be ashamed to call you His child.

CHAPTER 7

You Cannot Out-Sin God's Grace

Jesus is in the business of setting us free, not putting us into more bondage. There are a few verses that some latch onto. And they say these verses indicate that we're not totally forgiven. Here again we'll see that context is our best friend for understanding Scripture. Further, God is communicating to us not two messages, but one: we're forgiven people.

Will Be Forgiven?

The first is found in James 5:15:

> And the prayer of faith will save the one who is sick, and the Lord will raise him up. And if he has committed sins, he will be forgiven.

James is talking about praying for those who are sick and

how to comfort them (5:14). The "if" in verse 15 is a possibility and is in question. James is saying that if this person has committed sins, then remind him that they are forgiven so he doesn't think his sin caused the sickness.

Put another way, James is reassuring them that their sickness is not a result of their sin because they're already forgiven. That's why James says we can confess our sins to one another (5:16). Notice that he doesn't say we confess our sins to God in order to be forgiven. Instead, we confess because we *are* forgiven.

James doesn't say, "If they've committed sins, make sure they confess those sins to God and ask God to forgive them—and oh, make sure also that they've forgiven others." No. He simply says if they've committed sins, they're forgiven. There's no condition to this forgiveness. It's presented as a cause and effect. For example, if I jump up, I'll come down. If I sin, I'll be forgiven, because what Jesus did was enough.

Thank God there are no conditions to His forgiveness. There are no strings attached. Instead, James is in agreement with the rest of the New Testament. Believers are forgiven!

Willful Sin?

There's one last passage that needs to be looked at in order to solidify our once-for-all forgiveness:

> If we go on sinning willfully after receiving the knowledge of the truth, there no longer remains a sacrifice for sins. (Hebrews 10:26 NASB)

Does this verse mean that we can out-sin God's forgiveness? Well, Romans 5:20 clearly says this cannot happen: "Where sin increased, grace abounded all the more." So, what does Hebrews 10 really mean?

Once again, context is our friend. Before we look at this passage and the surrounding verses, it's critical to know who the writer of Hebrews is talking to in this section.

Hebrews 10:27 says that God will consume His adversaries or enemies. Also, in verse 39 of the same chapter, the writer says, "But we are not of those who shrink back and are destroyed, but of those who have faith and preserve their souls." If you're in Christ, then you do not shrink back because God will both finish what He started in you (Philippians 1:6) and present you blameless before Him (Jude 24). It seems clear then that the writer is addressing those who are not saved.

The only sin mentioned in Hebrews from chapters

1-10 is the sin of unbelief (Hebrews 3:18-19). The present participle of "willful" suggests the continuation of sin with no belief in Jesus.[12] Thus, the writer of Hebrews is writing to those who are continually rejecting God, which is why verse 27 says that they're God's enemies. For this reason, there is no sacrifice remaining for them (10:26), because they're rejecting the only sacrifice that can save them.

It's important to note that believers commit willful sin. All sin is willful. We choose to sin. I've never accidentally sinned. What the writer is talking about in this passage is the willful rejection of Jesus Christ as Savior.

The writer then compares the punishment between the law and the new covenant by asking a rhetorical question to all the audience. The writer says,

> How much more severe a punishment do you think that person deserves who tramples on God's Son, treats as common the blood of the covenant by which it was sanctified, and insults the Spirit of grace? (Hebrews 10:29 ISV)

This isn't meant to scare Christians, as if we could lose what God has given us. But this is a rhetorical question to contrast what those who willfully reject Christ deserve compared to those who rejected the law.

Some translations say "by which he was sanctified." The reason I chose this translation is because I believe it rightly understands the grammar and sentence structure of the original language. In the original language, covenant in this verse is the subject of the word sanctified.[13] The covenant has been set apart by Christ' blood. And the unbelieving person in view says the blood is simply "common," and not enough to forgive and save.

In summary, you cannot lose your salvation. You commit willful sins, but the willful sin in this passage speaks of the sin of rejecting Jesus. This passage is dealing with unbelievers and is not speaking to you. You have been forgiven of all your sins. And you are safe and secure in Jesus.

Confident in Our Walk

God's attitude toward us doesn't change when we sin. Yes, we still sin. We choose to do it every day. Sometimes it feels like we want to sin. Other times, we try so hard not to. Either way, our walk—good or bad—does not determine God's attitude toward us.

Our forgiveness means we can have confidence in each moment. This confidence is total trust that what Jesus did was enough, no matter what you feel in a given moment.

We don't have to stay in our shame or guilt. We're free to

bask in God's love and enjoy Him in every moment. When we sin, we can be confident that God is still within us, for us, and in love with us because the cross is still enough. Your sin did not surprise God, He saw it coming, yet He chose to walk with you through it because He cares for you.

You are forgiven. You are safe in God's hand (John 10:29). Nothing can separate you from His love (Romans 8:39). And no sin is too much for His grace (Romans 5:20).

CHAPTER 8

What Happens When We Sin?

We spend the rest of our lives learning about what it means to be totally forgiven. This is growth—learning to trust Jesus; learning to depend on Him even when we don't feel it. God is leading us to reinterpret our thoughts through what He has done for us and to us. This includes what we do when we sin. Instead of begging and pleading with God for something we already have, we can simply agree with Him and trust that we're good to go.

Repentance

Repentance is a beautiful and amazing thing in the Christian life. By repentance, I mean change of mind. This change of mind also leads to a change of behavior, but first and foremost, it's a change in our thinking and beliefs. Repentance is a result of God's pursuit of us. It's God's kindness that leads us to repentance (Romans 2:4). It's not our repentance that leads to God's kindness.

When we look at the New Testament, repentance is often connected with initial belief in the gospel. For example, God wishes that all should reach repentance and not perish (2 Peter 3:9). Further, Scripture says repentance "leads to life" (Acts 11:18), "leads to salvation" (2 Corinthians 7:10) and leads "to a knowledge of the truth" (2 Timothy 2:25). Over and over again in the book of Acts, unbelievers are called to repent and turn to God (Acts 2:38; 3:19; 8:22; 17:30; 26:20).

Repentance is also for the believer. We're called to be transformed by the renewing of our mind (Romans 12:2), to think on things above (Colossians 3:2), to fix our eyes on Jesus (Hebrews 12:2), and to take every thought captive so that we can obey Christ (2 Corinthians 10:5). So repentance isn't about getting more forgiveness from God, but about changing the way we think in a given moment.

When we sin, instead of confessing every sin or asking God to forgive us, we can repent! When we sin, we can make the choice that sin is no good and turn from it. As new creations, this is our new heart's desire. It makes no sense for us to linger in sin, because we're not made for it.

Next time you sin, turn from it, fix your eyes on Jesus, and be reminded that you're forgiven and loved. It's only when we look to Jesus that our minds are changed (repentance), and we're reminded that what He has done for us really worked.

Sorrow and Regret

Let me say from the outset, sorrow and regret over sin is good and healthy for the believer. Just because we're forgiven of all sins doesn't mean we don't hate it when we sin. Although feeling sorrow and regret over sin is a good sign that Christ lives in you, what lead God to forgive us was not our sorrow and regret, but Christ's blood..

However, dwelling in your sorrow and regret for long periods of time doesn't produce anything that's healthy. Sure, when you sin, it's okay to feel sorrow and regret, but you don't have to live in this. Instead, we can choose to forget what lies behind us and focus on the goal of knowing Christ (Philippians 3:8-13). There's a balance between feeling sorrow and regret over sin and living in the confidence that Jesus has forgiven you.

We're not called to beat ourselves up over our sin. We can choose to agree with God that He has taken away and forgotten our sins forever. God isn't asking us to dwell on the past. God is asking us to focus on His Son.

Grieving and Quenching the Spirit

Although we're forgiven of all sins, we can still grieve the Spirit and quench the Spirit. Ephesians 4:30 tells us not to grieve the Holy Spirit. This doesn't mean that the Holy Spirit is mad at you or has left you. God promises to never again be angry with us (Isaiah 54:9), and to never leave us (Hebrews 13:5). Further, we've been sealed with the Spirit (Ephesians 1:13). He's not going anywhere!

Grieving the Spirit happens when we sin and do not express Him. The Spirit is grieved because He hates when we sin. Sin hurts us. The Spirit wants what's best for us, and sin is not what is best for us.

Although Jesus has taken all the punishment for our sin, sin can still have real earthly consequences. For example, if I choose to get drunk, then I am harming my body and potentially those around me. These consequences are not coming from God, but from my own choices.

If I were to tell my little brother not to touch the burning stove and he did, I would be grieved. I would be grieved because he did something that wasn't good for him and that actually harmed him. This is why we can trust that the Spirit will never lead us to sin. He is always leading us to the truth that sets us free.

The Spirit grieving when we sin shows the care and

compassion that God has for us. It also reveals that our behavior matters to God. Our behavior doesn't make us any more forgiven or accepted by God. But God cares about us and is teaching us to say no to sin (Titus 2:12). He cares about what we do because He loves us. He does not want us to sin, but to find life in trusting Him.

God cares about our behavior because He cares about us. He's not a new covenant robot that doesn't care about the choices we make. No, He wants us to live fulfilled lives. And this happens only by living out of who we are in Him. We were re-created to live godly lives. And sin is the last thing that brings satisfaction to us. We're satisfied only when we trust in Jesus.

Paul picks up this same theme in 1 Thessalonians 5:19 when he tells the church not to "quench the Spirit." This happens when we sin. We quench the Spirit by not trusting in the Spirit to live through us. When we walk after sin and the flesh, we aren't walking by the Spirit, and thus we aren't expressing Him.

Once again, this doesn't mean the Spirit leaves us, and it doesn't mean we're not in the Spirit. Our position in Christ and in the Spirit is always the same (Romans 8:9). That's why when we sin, the Spirit goes with us. This means that we are in the Spirit when we sin. For this reason, it's possible for us to quench or grieve the Spirit.

The Spirit Cares

The Holy Spirit cares about you. He'll never lead you in the direction of sin. And He is more than enough to guide and lead you into all truth. He cares about you. He knows that sin isn't good for you. It never pays off. The Holy Spirit wants you to live the life that God has fashioned you to live. You're meant to trust Jesus. You're designed to walk by His Spirit. When you do this, you find true fulfillment and satisfaction.

But even when you don't, the Holy Spirit keeps reminding you of your forgiveness, purity, and cleansing in Christ. The Holy Spirit is teaching you that there's nothing wrong with you. No matter where you go or how you walk, He is always guiding, comforting, and teaching you.

CHAPTER 9

Conviction and Communion

When I hear believers say that the Holy Spirit is convicting them of their sins, I want to say, "Wait—you're telling me that the Holy Spirit is declaring you guilty for your sins and sentencing you to punishment?" That of course is what the word *convict* means. Is the Spirit really convicting believers of something Jesus has already taken away?

There's only one verse around this idea of the Holy Spirit and conviction. It is found in John 16. In context, Jesus is talking about the Holy Spirit and what He will come to do when He leaves. Notice in this passage who the Holy Spirit convicts and what it concerns:

> And when he comes, he will convict the world concerning sin and righteousness and judgment: concerning sin, because they do not believe in me; concerning righteousness, because I go to the Father, and you will see me no longer; concerning judgment, because the ruler of this world is judged. (John 16:8-11)

The Holy Spirit convicts the world of sin, righteousness, and judgment. "Convict" here means to declare guilty or to expose. The Holy Spirit is convicting the world of their sin of unbelief, so they can see their need for belief in Jesus (16:9). The Holy Spirit is convicting the world of their righteousness, which is filthy rags in comparison to God's righteousness. And the Holy Spirit is convicting the world of their wrong judgment of who Christ is. On the cross, the world thought they were judging Christ, but Satan—the "ruler of this world"—was being judged.[14]

The Holy Spirit is not convicting believers of sin, because we're not convicts. Jesus was convicted for our sin. The punishment was death. He died. Now we no longer have to pay the wages for our sin or be convicted for them. God will not convict us for something He already convicted at the cross.

Believers are not convicts. We are children. And God isn't treating us like guilty criminals. Jesus became our sin and guilt, so that we could become His righteousness (2 Corinthians 5:21). We no longer stand guilty or condemned because Jesus became our sin. The Spirit is not convicting us of what Jesus has taken away. He is not making us feel guilt or shame over our sins. Instead, He's reminding us of all Jesus did to take away our guilt and shame.

Scripture says the Holy Spirit is teaching us all things (John 14:26), testifying about Christ (John 15:26), and guiding us into all truth (John 16:13)—not convicting us for something Jesus already dealt with.

Put simply, the Holy Spirit is teaching you the truth about your forgiveness. He's testifying about the Savior who took away your sin. And He's leading you into the truth that always sets you free!

In addition, the Holy Spirit is bearing witness to us that God remembers our sins no more:

> And the Holy Spirit also bears witness to us; for after saying... I will remember their sins and their lawless deeds no more. (Hebrews 10:15-17)

The Father, the Son, and the Holy Spirit all agree that the cross worked, and you are totally forgiven!

Unworthy Manner?

Growing up, the Lord's Supper was always a time of examining my past and feeling bad about myself. The lights were dimmed, and the preacher always made us make sure we were "right" with God before taking the elements. Have you experienced this? In most churches, instead of celebrating and remembering Christ, the Lord's Supper is about feeling condemned and remembering our sin.

As we'll see in 1 Corinthians, the Lord's Supper is about remembering and celebrating all that Christ did to make us forgiven and right with Him. We don't have to make sure we're right with God before we take it, because we can trust that we're right with God forever (Romans 5:1). Further, we don't have to focus on our sins during the Lord's Supper. Instead, we get to focus on Jesus and what He did to take away our sins.

Put simply, the Lord's Supper isn't about us; it's all about Jesus. It's not about remembering our sin but about remembering our Savior who took away our sin.

The "unworthy manner" in 1 Corinthians 11:27 is not about having unconfessed sin or not being right with God. Taking the Lord's Supper in an unworthy manner means not respecting the Lord's Supper. It means using the elements in a way that doesn't remember or celebrate Jesus.

In context, Paul is trying to create order in the Corinthian church during the Lord's Supper. There were people who were taking the Lord's Supper as a meal (11:20). And some members became weak and ill (11:30) because they used the wine to get drunk (11:21). This is why those who do this are "guilty concerning the body and blood of the Lord" (11:27). They've sinned by disrespecting God and this celebration.

This is why Paul tells the believers to examine themselves (11:28). This isn't about examining your history of sin or getting right with God. Instead, this is about making sure you're not disrespecting the Lord's Supper by eating it as a meal or getting drunk off of the wine. Paul is telling them to examine whether they're taking the Lord's Supper in a worthy manner. To take it in a worthy manner is to celebrate and remember Jesus, not use it as a meal or an opportunity for drunkenness.

Paul moves on to say that those who haven't discerned what they're doing have placed judgment on themselves (11:29). This judgment is not from God, but from others. They've sinned and are now judged (found guilty) from the rest of the community. Since they haven't discerned the purpose of the Lord's Supper, they are ill, and some have died (11:30).

These are the results of "drinking judgment on themselves" (11:29). They abused the Lord's Supper so much that they got sick, and as a result, everyone realized what they were doing. That's what it means to drink judgment on themselves.

Notice that these things are not from God, but from the choices people made to abuse the Lord's Supper. They were eating too much and getting drunk to the point that they were getting sick and dying! This will help give us context for the next few verses that speak on judgment. God isn't making us sick or killing us because of sin. The wages of sin is death. Jesus died and took our punishment so that we wouldn't have to.

In verse 31, Paul says those who discern or judge themselves would not be judged. Once again, this means they would not be found guilty from others for abusing the Lord's Supper and would not have to suffer the consequences of getting drunk. If these people would just discern what they were doing, they would not be judged by others.

"But when we are judged..." (11:32)—who are we judged by? Others. When people come and tell us that what we're doing is wrong, we're being judged.[15] This doesn't mean others are convicting us, but they're discerning (judging) our behavior and saying that it's wrong. This is how God disciplines (trains) us. He uses others to confront us, not shame us, so that we can learn the truth about a matter.

The verse goes on to say, "But when we are judged, we are disciplined by the Lord so that we will not be condemned along with the world" (1 Corinthians 11:32 NASB). This means that God uses others to discipline us. Discipline here means to teach and train. As we'll see later,

God's discipline is not about punishment for our sins.

God disciplines us so that we won't be condemned along with the world. This means He wants us to not look like the rest of the world. This condemnation will never happen but is mentioned here to contrast those who are saved with those who are not. Those who are saved are under God's discipline, and those who are not saved are condemned already.

Some translations say, "when we are judged by the Lord..." But the structure of the original language simply has "when we are judged." In context, the judgment is not coming from God, but from others.

That's why the passage goes on to say we should wait for one another and eat at home "so that you will not come together for judgment" (1 Corinthians 11:34 NASB). Paul's advice is to eat at home so that you don't take the Lord's Supper as a meal and be judged by others.

Comfort and Training

The Holy Spirit is not convicting you, but comforting you. He's not putting you on trial for each sin. He's reminding you that you're forgiven of all sin. The Holy Spirit is not making us feel dirty. He's reminding us that we're clean.

So next time you get those thoughts, know that they're

not coming from God. He is constantly showing you that you're clean, close to Him, and forgiven.

This comfort also means training. God is able to teach us and train us through everything we go through so that in the future we can trust Him. He's always teaching and training us. He isn't punishing us for our past, nor is His discipline a reaction to our sin. Since He loves us, He's always disciplining us.

Remember, there will never be condemnation for us (Romans 8:1). And we are always under the loving discipline of our heavenly Father. We can trust His discipline because He is good, and He is for us.

REASON 2

YOU'RE JUST LIKE JESUS

CHAPTER 10

No More Tears

There you are, standing face to face with Jesus. Does this scare you? What do you think of when you picture the final judgment? Is Jesus looking at you with disgust?

Many of us have been taught that when we appear in front of Jesus on that day, there'll be a movie of our life for all to see. But is this what Scripture describes? And how does understanding our total forgiveness change the way we understand judgment?

God is not keeping a record of our wrongs in order to get us back on judgment day. No, He destroyed the record once and for all. Since God has forgiven us of all our sins, we can be confident on the day of judgment.

One Judgment or Two?

Everyone, both believer and unbeliever, will appear at the final judgment (2 Corinthians 5:10; Romans 14:10; 1 Peter 4:17a; Matthew 12:36). However, some argue that there are two judgments; one for believers and one for unbelievers. I think the premise of the following chapters can still be true for those who hold to that view. But usually those who hold to that view teach that God is rewarding believers with many rewards and special honors.

Those who say there are two judgments make a distinction between the judgment seat of Christ and the final judgment. They say Christians will appear at the judgment seat of Christ to collect their rewards, and unbelievers will appear at the final judgment to get their eternal sentence.

However, Scripture never makes this distinction. Although there's mention of the judgment seat of Christ, believers and unbelievers are always in view. The final judgment and the judgment seat of Christ are the same event. Understanding this is important, because the final judgment is black and white. If you're saved, then you're rewarded the same as others who are saved. And if you are lost, then you're condemned the same as others who are lost.

Paul mentions the judgment seat of Christ in two places—Romans 14:10 and 2 Corinthians 5:10. In Romans 14:10, he says that "we will all stand before the judgment seat of Christ." Notice that he says "all" will stand before the judgment seat, not just believers. He identifies the "all" of verse 10 in the next verse:

For it is written, "As I live, says the Lord, every knee shall bow to me, and every tongue shall confess to God." (Romans 14:11)

It seems clear—based on the context of Romans 14—that everyone will appear before the judgment seat.

The next and only other mention of the judgment seat is in 2 Corinthians 5:10. Paul says:

For we must all appear before the judgment seat of Christ, so that each one may receive what is due for what he has done in the body, whether good or evil.

Once again, he says all, not just believers. If this was just talking about believers, how could believers receive evil if Jesus has taken away all the evil? As we see in context, Paul says this to "persuade others" (2 Corinthians 5:11), and for the goal of seeing unbelievers become reconciled to God (2 Corinthians 5:20).

Further, he says in verse 21 that Jesus has become our sin so that we might become His righteousness. Clearly then, 2 Corinthians 5:10 is simply revealing that all will appear before God. Believers and unbelievers will receive what is due them—eternal life or eternal separation from God.

In summary, a single judgment is the clear picture in

the entire New Testament. In Revelation 20-21, the great white throne judgment speaks of both unbelievers and believers appearing (Revelation 20:11-15; 21:6-8).

In Matthew 25:31-46, Jesus reveals that at the final judgment, He will separate the goats (unbelievers) from the sheep (believers). There is no mention of believers appearing at a different time; instead, all will appear at the same time. And as we'll see, all will be rewarded the same.

We shouldn't get caught up or be worried about what will happen in the end times. When you read the book of Revelation, know that it's primarily a symbolic book revealing to us who God is and His victory over sin, death, and the enemy. The book of Revelation is meant to give us hope that no matter what our circumstances look like, we win!

What to Expect

Believers can anticipate that they'll be treated like Jesus on the day of judgment. We will not be judged for our sins, nor will God even mention them or bring them up. We can have confidence that we will not be judged for our sins because what Jesus did for us… worked!

1 John 4:17 gives us complete assurance and confidence on the day of judgment:

By this is love perfected with us, so that we may have confidence for the day of judgment, because as he is so also are we in this world.

Why can we have confidence? Because we're like Jesus. This doesn't mean we *are* Jesus; instead this means that we are as righteous, accepted, and holy as Jesus is. This is echoed in 1 Corinthians 1:30 when Paul says that Jesus is our "righteousness, holiness, and redemption."

The gospel is that Jesus was judged for our sins so that we would never have to be judged for them. He took what we deserved so that we could get what He deserved. That is grace. That is the gospel. That's why we can have confidence on judgment day.

What's even more comforting for us is that Jesus will be the final judge (Acts 17:31; John 5:22, 27; 2 Timothy 4:1). Do you really think that after becoming our sin and taking the punishment for our sin, He would really judge us again? No way! That's why when He returns, He will not deal with our sin (Hebrews 9:28). He is for us!

There'll be no film of our sins at the final judgment, nor is God going to pull out our record of sins. Jesus has forgiven us all our sins "by canceling the record of debt that stood against us with its legal demands. This he set aside, nailing it to the cross" (Colossians 2:13).

The film—it's destroyed. The record—it's torn up. God remembers our sins no more (Hebrews 8:12) and will never bring our sins up again.

This is why we read in John 3:18 (NASB) that the person "who believes in Him is not judged." All those who believe will be saved and will not perish (John 3:16). Therefore, they will not be judged for their sin, and they will be saved.

Jesus solidifies this thought in John 5:24 (NASB):

> Truly, truly, I say to you, he who hears My word, and believes Him who sent Me, has eternal life, and does not come into judgment, but has passed out of death into life.

The "judgment" in this verse is judgment for sin. We will not be judged for our sins because we believe in Jesus, have eternal life, and have passed out of death into life.

This is why the apostle Paul can confidently say, "There is therefore now no condemnation for those who are in Christ Jesus" (Romans 8:1). There's no condemnation for our sins, and there never will be. Why? Because God has already condemned sin in the body of Jesus (Romans 8:3). There's no condemnation left.

He is not condemning you for your sin now, nor will

He condemn you for your sin at the final judgment. God's grace does not stop at the gates of heaven. What He's saying now in His word is what He will say at the final judgment. He is the same yesterday, today, and forever (Hebrews 13:8).

Christ has accepted us (Romans 15:7). We're not seeking to earn this acceptance. It's already ours. This is why on the day of judgment we can be confident knowing that He will confirm His acceptance of us. Further, we are a pleasing aroma to God (2 Corinthians 2:15) because He is not mad at us (Isaiah 54:9).

We are blameless (Colossians 1:22; Jude 1:24; 1 Thessalonians 5:23). This means that we are innocent. This innocence is rooted in the person and the finished work of Jesus. And Jesus, the One who will judge us, is also the One who'll present us as blameless:

> Now to him who is able to keep you from stumbling and to present you blameless before the presence of his glory with great joy. (Jude 24)

> He has now reconciled in his body of flesh by his death, in order to present you holy and blameless and above reproach before him. (Colossians 1:22)

Do you see why you can have confidence? You are totally

forgiven, perfectly clean, blameless, and accepted, just like Jesus! There's no reason to fear. Jesus will be welcoming you with open arms.

When you see Jesus face to face, expect a smile. A hug. And no judgment for your sins! In the coming chapters, we'll look at verses concerning judgment, and discover why we can really have confidence. But next, we will look at what else we can expect.

CHAPTER 11

Jesus Is Our Reward

The popular notion in Christian circles today is that we're saved by grace but rewarded by works. Many people claim that how we live on earth will determine how much we enjoy of heaven. These people speak of varying degrees of enjoyment and varying degrees of rewards.

However, as we'll see in the next section, the Scripture never uses the plural word *rewards* to talk about what we will get. Instead, the singular word *reward* is used. Further, God has one way of dealing with His people—unconditional grace. This means that we all get what we don't deserve because Jesus took what we did deserve.

I don't think that Christians will be rewarded differently based on their works, or be distinguished from one another based on their works. I believe that when we look at the texts on reward, we'll see a clear picture: *Jesus* is our reward, and no other reward matters.

Further, the apostle Paul considered everything else

worthless next to knowing Christ (Philippians 3:8). His only goal was Christ (Philippians 3:14). In light of this, how do we understand reward?

Reward and Crown

The story of the vineyard workers found in Matthew 20:1-15 is the story of workers showing up at different times, working different amounts, and all getting paid the same. The boss of the vineyard agreed to a pay the first set of workers a day's wage (20:2). However, the boss kept hiring more workers every three hours (20:3-6). At the end of the day, he hired some workers with only one hour left in the day (20:7). He then told his foreman to call up all the hired hands and to pay them all the same amount, beginning with the last workers hired (20:8-10).

The workers who worked all day said, "This is unfair!" However, this is God's way of grace. Everyone is treated the same and at the same time. That is fair! Everyone is equal in God's kingdom, which means our motivation to work for God is not in what He will give us, but is based on what He has already given us in Christ.

So whether you were saved when you were six or saved on your death bed, according to this parable, we all get rewarded the same. That's the meaning of Jesus's saying,

"The last will be first, and the first last." He's saying there's no merit involved and no ranking. It's all by grace. As we'll see, if Jesus is our reward, then we all get over paid, no matter how much we worked.

When we scan the rest of the New Testament, we see the idea of reward and different crowns. As we'll see, the context for both reward and crown speak of our eternal life and eternal reward—Jesus Christ.

There are five passages that speak of a crown believers will receive. It's worth noting that a majority of scholars agree that "crown" symbolizes what awaits us: eternal life, not varying degrees of reward.[16] Further, most scholars agree that the crown in these passages is not a literal crown.[17]

For example, 2 Timothy 4:8 says all believers, not some, will get a crown of righteousness. James 1:12 and Revelation 2:10 says we'll receive a "crown of life." And in 1 Thessalonians 2:19, Paul speaks about a "crown of boasting."

None of the above verses say that this crown is received based on works; nor do they say they're given to only some believers. Further, are we going to stack these crowns on our head? No. As we look at each one, we see how they point to our eternal life, which is a Person, Jesus Christ. Jesus is our righteousness (2 Corinthians 5:21), Jesus is our life (Colossians 3:3-4), and Jesus is the one we boast in (1

YOU'RE JUST LIKE JESUS

Corinthians 1:29; Galatians 6:14).

1 Peter 5:4 mentions elders receiving a crown of glory. Based on the other texts centered on crowns, this verse is a promise that elders will receive eternal life. Not only that, but they'll have the eternal satisfaction of being an example to the flock (1 Peter 5:3).

Further, in heaven, we get to fully enjoy His righteousness with no sin to hinder that. We get to enjoy His physical life and presence, which includes His glory. And we get to boast for all eternity of what He has done for us, to us, and through us.

There's mention in Revelation of twenty-four elders casting their crowns before God's throne (Revelation 4:10), but they do not keep the crowns, nor is it mentioned how they got them. It's also worth noting that all of Revelation is symbolic of something. This picture of elders casting their crowns before God's throne is most likely an image of their casting everything they have to God. Nonetheless, this imagery proves that all believers in heaven are of equal status.

As we look at the various reward passages, note that none speak of varying rewards, and all speak of a singular reward. None of the passages relating to reward say that only certain believers will receive them (Revelation 22:12;

Revelation 11:18; 2 John 1:8; Mark 9:41; Luke 6:23, 35).

In Matthew, Jesus often speaks of the concept of reward (Matthew 5:10, 12, 46; 6:1-2, 4, 6, 16, 18; 10:41-42). In all these references, Jesus's words are an encouragement to believers, or they contrast the reward that believers will receive with what those who do not believe will receive. In Matthew we read about a "reward in full" (NASB) or a reward that is "great in heaven," but both phrases speak of the result of believing in Christ.

Jesus speaks of a treasure laid up in heaven (Matthew 6:20). But treasures are discovered, not worked for like rewards. Jesus is telling us that our daily choices matter and that they'll be eternal, since they're expressions of Him.

Paul says that our reward is our inheritance: "From the Lord you will receive the inheritance as your reward" (Colossians 3:24). You do not work for or earn an inheritance. It's freely given to you because you're part of the family.

Paul also mentions a prize we get for finishing the race (1 Corinthians 9:25) but contrasts that with those who do not run. The prize is eternal life. The prize is Christ. The reward is the amazing opportunity to be with and know Jesus for all eternity. Our reward is given to us because we believe in Jesus, not because we do good or run well.

Treated Like Jesus!

So what can we expect when we see Jesus face to face?

- No judgment for our sins. And no film of our sins.
- We will receive the greatest reward—Jesus Christ.
- We can expect to be treated like Jesus.

Yes, we have Him living in us now, but in heaven we'll be with His physical self, in His presence. As Paul said, "to live is Christ and to die is gain" (Philippians 1:21). Our reward is Jesus. And everything else is worthless next to knowing Christ.

Further, God's grace is the same yesterday, today, and for all eternity. As believers, we're blessed with every spiritual blessing (Ephesians 1:3) the moment we believe in Jesus. God does not bless us on earth for what we do for Him. Instead, He has given each of us the best He has by giving us His Son. We live from God's blessing, not for it. We live from God's unconditional approval of us, not for it.

Jesus took the treatment we deserved so that we could take the treatment that He deserves. We will be treated like Jesus because "as he is so also are we in this world" (1 John 4:17). For the rest of your life, God will treat you like Jesus. Is Jesus accepted, pleasing, and loved by God?

Then you are accepted, pleasing, and loved by God. Is Jesus being punished, shamed, or condemned by God? No. Therefore, you will never be punished, shamed, or condemned by God.

In the same way that God blesses us the same, He rewards us all the same. So there'll be no comparison of rewards, because we'll all be rewarded the same. Our reward is based on Jesus's work for us, not our works for Him.

There'll no more tears, no more shame, and no more pain (Revelation 21:4). For all eternity, we get to know Jesus more. Thank you, Jesus, for the amazing reward you are.

The pressure's off. We get to simply know and enjoy Jesus without the pressure of having to perform for Him.

CHAPTER 12

No More Fear

In this chapter, we'll take a closer look at some of the verses that talk about judgment day. If we're all getting the same reward, then how do our works play into the final judgment?

We'll see that we're not rewarded because of our works; instead God judges our works to see which ones will last for eternity. As we saw in the last chapter, we can have confidence, not fear, on the day of judgment. As we look at these passages, we'll see the simple truth about judgment and why we can truly have no fear.

Great White Throne

The great white throne judgment found in Revelation 20 and 21 is a black and white judgment. You're either saved and going to heaven, or not saved and cast into the lake of fire. It's critical to understand that there are also no levels of punishment in hell. The punishment is eternal separation from God. I say this because we'll see in Revelation 20 that they were judged according to their deeds, but they all got the same punishment. This will help us understand this phrase later in regard to our reward and judgment.

Revelation 20:12-13 says those who are dead are judged according to what they did, and they, along with death and hades, are thrown into the lake of fire (20:14-15). Their names were not in the book of life. Therefore, they were unbelievers and were cast into hell.

In contrast, Revelation 21 is all about believers. A loud voice announces that God will dwell with His people and will wipe away all tears, pain, mourning, and crying (21:3-4). Then God says, "The one who conquers will have this heritage, and I will be his God and he will be my son" (21:7).

How do we conquer? Through the blood of the Lamb (Revelation 12:11). Not only that, but through Jesus, we're called "more than conquerors" (Romans 8:37). He contrasts this with verse 8 that speaks of unbelievers. There's also no mention of varying rewards or inheritances. We all get the same thing. We all receive a heritage or inheritance because we're part of the family; it isn't given based on works.

Sound like we should fear the great white throne judgment? No! We can expect to be with God, and to have Him take away any fear, shame, and pain. He will announce on that day that we are His beloved children.

Sheep and Goats

In Matthew 25, Matthew speaks of the final judgment and what Jesus will do. As Jesus sits on His throne, He will separate people one from another. "He will place the sheep on his right, but the goats on the left" (Matthew 25:32). The sheep represent believers and the goats represent unbelievers.

For this reason, He will say to those on the right (the sheep), "Come, you who are blessed by my Father, inherit the kingdom prepared for you from the foundation of the world" (25:34). Then he lists off things we did for him (25:35-36). Notice that we all get the same thing, no matter what we did. There's no mention in this section of varying degrees of rewards. Instead, we receive an inheritance because we're part of the family. Our reward is our inheritance.

Then he says to those on the left (the goats), "Depart from me, you cursed, into the eternal fire prepared for the devil and his angels" (25:41). He then lists of the bad things they did (25:42-43). Notice, no matter what they did, they all got punished the same.

Matthew ends this section of Scripture with a summary and contrast of believers and unbelievers. He says, "And these [goats] will go away into eternal punishment, but the righteous [sheep] into eternal life" (25:46).

This is not a grey issue. It's black and white. You're either saved and receive eternal life, or not saved and go away into eternal punishment. All believers receive the same thing and all unbelievers receive the same thing.

Anxious for Nothing

Anxiety haunts us all. Fear of the future. Fear of wanting everything to go just right. Our total forgiveness means we can have confidence that when we die, Jesus will welcome us with open arms. Our total forgiveness means we can look ahead knowing that no matter what happens tomorrow or next week, we are safe and secure in Jesus.

Paul says that the moment we die, we will be present with the Lord (2 Corinthians 5:8). Death can be an exciting thing because we know what will happen. We'll be with Jesus. There'll be no more pain or shame. Every anxious thought will be gone.

We can trust Jesus. We can give Him all our fear and anxiety. Why? Because He cares for us (1 Peter 5:7). What does this look like? For me, it means telling Him what I am going through and telling Him what I am fearful of.

God is not judging, condemning you, or shaking His head at you. He is within you. He cares for you. And He wants you to have confidence that He has forgiven you.

CHAPTER 13

Judgment by Works?

When God judges our works, He is not judging them to determine the rewards we'll get or the status we'll earn in heaven. Instead, He's simply seeing which ones were done in dependence on Him and which were not. Those that were good will be celebrated for all eternity because they were expressions of Jesus. And those that were bad have been taken away once and for all.

Built on Christ

In 1 Corinthians 3, Paul is talking about laying a foundation on Christ and the benefit such an act has. Specifically, he's referring to building a doctrine that is on Christ. As we look at these verses, it's important to note that Paul never says we collect many rewards; instead, he simply says we will receive a reward (3:8, 14).

Paul, comparing his work to that done by Apollos, says that their work did not matter since it is God who causes the growth (3:5-7). He then says that no matter who did what, they both receive a reward according to their labor.

Now, in this first instance, it seems that "reward" is not the reward they will get on judgment day. Rather, this refers to the personal reward they get in participating in God's work in the Corinthian church. This is why Paul mentions later that his reward is preaching the gospel without charge (1 Corinthians 9:18).

Nonetheless, for Paul, our reward is our inheritance (Colossians 3:24), and we get to celebrate for all eternity the work God did through us. This in itself is a reward. Paul seems to be talking about teachers who either build their doctrine on Christ and those who do not. Either way, the message is the same.

Paul moves on to say that each man should all build on Christ because if they do not, it will become evident on judgment day (1 Corinthians 3:10-13). Paul says that if the work they built on Christ remains, then they will receive a reward. Here it seems that the reward is the eternal celebration that they got to participate in God's work. Further, the reward is that they did not have wasted time, but instead built things that lasted eternally.

Paul contrasts this with verse 15 by saying that if anyone's work is burned up, he will suffer loss. What is the loss here? The loss is not having work that is eternal; that's why he says the person is still saved. They wasted time not building their work on Christ. This is not about eternal shame and sadness, or varying degrees of rewards.

Whether this passage is specifically dealing with teachers or all believers, we can know that our work built on Christ does matter, because it's a work of God through us that will be celebrated for all eternity.

So the reward in this passage is not more square footage or jewelry. The reward is the satisfaction of participating with God in our lives now. Just like today, when you look back to the time you helped someone, it feels good. The reward is the experience. And for all of eternity we will celebrate the moments we trusted Christ to live His life through us.

Further, he moves on to say that when God does judge us, we will each receive praise from Him (1 Corinthians 4:5). Once again, this is not varying degrees of rewards, but simply a recognition that God loves us.

Understanding Judgment of Works

In 2 Corinthians 5:10 we read that all will receive what is due to them according to the deeds they did—whether good or evil. Paul is saying that if one has done good (believed in Jesus), that person will receive what is due—eternal life. If one has done evil (rejected Jesus), he will receive eternal punishment. This is echoed in Revelation 22:12. Here, God is going to give out what we have done. Have we believed in Jesus or have we rejected Him? If we've believed, then He is our reward.

In Paul's theology, we are saved by grace, not by works, which is why he calls our reward an inheritance. We already know that we will not be judged for our sins, which is why 2 Corinthians 5:10 is a contrast between believers and unbelievers.

In Romans 2, Paul mentions that the world is judged according to their deeds (Romans 2:6), and that God will judge the secrets of men (Romans 2:16). Once again, context is our best friend in order to understand what Paul is talking about.

In Romans 2:7-8, Paul says that anyone who does good can earn eternal life, and those who do bad will get wrath and fury. Paul then says that there is no partiality with God (2:11). Essentially in chapter 2 he's saying that if you want to live by the law or live by morality, go for it—but God will judge you according to that.

If anybody wondered if they could do this, Paul goes on to say in Romans 3:11-12 that there is no one who does good, no one who is righteous, and no one who seeks God. So the judgment found in Romans 2 is not about believers; instead Paul is making his case that salvation is by grace alone through faith alone. Further, the judgment in Romans 2 is about whether one is saved. And everyone in Romans 2 is *not* saved, because no one can earn salvation through what they do.

Paul says that all of us have fallen short of God's standard; but—thank God!—we are made right as a gift by His grace through what Jesus did (Romans 3:23-24). Paul goes on to say that we are made right by faith apart from works (Romans 3:28; 5:1). Later, in Romans 11:6, he says that "if it is by grace, it is no longer on the basis of works; otherwise grace would no longer be grace."

It's clear to Paul that we're saved by grace, and that our salvation isn't based on works. This is why we can have confidence before God because our salvation is not based on what we do but on what Jesus has done for us.

1 Peter 1:17 says that God judges according to each one's deeds. In context, Peter is encouraging the church to live holy (1:16). Why? Because what they do matters. He's not talking about living holy in order to earn eternal salvation. He clears that up in verses 18-19 by saying we were redeemed "by the precious blood of Christ."

Peter is saying God is discerning (judging) our works; the ones that are bad are taken away, and the ones that are good are celebrated forever. Nothing in this passage speaks of varying degrees of rewards or punishment, but just the plain truth that what we do matters.

Your Works Matter

The good works we do are not wasted time, but will be remembered and celebrated for all eternity. However, our good works do not determine our reward or our place in heaven. Instead, we're all rewarded the same, because it's all by grace. God judges our works to determine which will be burned up and which will last forever.

This means it's not about having more good works, or worrying about whether you have enough. You get to simply live without worrying if you're doing enough. Remember, Christ has already done *all* the work that needed to be done to make you accepted, forgiven, and right with God. That's why the good works we do are all because we love God and want to participate in His work each day.

CHAPTER 14

God Is Not an Accountant

There are a few verses in the New Testament that speak of us giving an account or having to give an account for everything we do. As we look at these passages, it's clear that they're contrasting saved and lost people, not different believers or different rewards. To "give an account" is to tell God if you believed in Him or not.

In Romans 14:12, Paul says that everyone will give an account of himself. The verse before said that everyone shall bow to God (14:11). Clearly then, Paul is saying at the judgment seat, will you say you believed in Jesus or rejected Him? He does not mention giving an account of everything we did, but in context is implying a question: Will you say you trusted Jesus or not?

Matthew 12:36-37 also uses this language and says that everyone will give an account for what they said. We have to understand what Matthew means by words. He says in verse 37 that we're either justified by our words or condemned by them.

Obviously, he's not talking about justification by works through the words we say. He's contrasting the believer and unbeliever by saying, "With your words, do you confess Jesus or do you reject Him?" This coincides with Romans 10:9: "If you confess with your mouth that Jesus is Lord and believe in your heart that God raised him from the dead, you will be saved."

This passage is not saying that we'll have to bring up every word that we say but is instead contrasting the believer and unbeliever. Once again, we will not be judged for the "bad" words we say because they've been taken away. And we know that everything good we say and do will last forever and will not be burned up.

Will Teachers Be Judged?

James 3:1 says that teachers will incur a stricter judgment. He spends the rest of the chapter talking about the power of the tongue and how hard it is to control. Since teachers held a high position in both the church and the society, James is warning that if one becomes a teacher, he'll be under strict judgment from others, which is why he should watch what he says.

For this reason, James says in verse 2, *"We all stumble in many ways.*" He's not talking about God's judgment, because we will not be judged for our stumbling (sin). Instead, James is talking about judgment from others, which is why we need to watch what we say and do. Put another way, since teachers are the leaders of the church, when they stumble, they'll be under stricter judgment from others than everyone else.

As we saw earlier, there is no separate judgment for teachers. There is one judgment. And those of us in Christ will not be judged for our sins and will all receive the same reward—Jesus Christ.

Did God Kill Ananias and Sapphira?

The story of Ananias and Sapphira lying about money and falling dead is found in Acts 5:1-11. As you read this story, you notice a few things. First, the passage never says that God killed them. Instead, it says they fell down and breathed their last (5:5, 11). Second, it never says that they're believers. Instead, it says that Satan filled Ananias's heart (5:3), and that his wife was in on it (5:9).

Now, Scripture says that believers have new hearts (Ezekiel 36:26), obedient hearts (Romans 6:17), and hearts filled with God's love (Romans 5:5). Additionally, Ephesians 3:17 says that Christ lives in our heart. Furthermore,

Satan cannot touch believers (1 John 5:18). This leads us to conclude that Ananias and Sapphira were not believers but were just a part of the church.

If this story was really about God striking down believers for sin, then we would all be dead. But that is not the gospel. The gospel is that Jesus took our sin and the punishment for our sin so that we would never have to!

All Eyes on Jesus

Instead of worrying about what we're doing, we get to fix our eyes on Jesus. Instead of trying to do more or be better, we get to simply enjoy our Father. Our total forgiveness means we're free to just be with Jesus without any pressure to do more for Him.

The standard has been met. The expectations were fulfilled. Now Jesus is asking us to sit down, kick up our feet, and trust in what He has done. The goal of the Christian life is not to do more things for God. The goal is to simply know Jesus.

God is not a task-master. And God is not your boss. He's your friend, your Savior, and your Father. He's not asking you to try harder, but to trust. After all, it's our trust, not our effort, that pleases Him (Hebrews 11:6).

CHAPTER 15

Faith Without Works

In this chapter, we'll discuss the motivation for good works in the Christian life. Further, we'll look at what James meant when he said that faith without works is dead. As we'll see in this chapter, our motivation to do good works comes from the presence of Christ in us and the glorious goal of getting to know Him more. Not only that, but we're designed to do good works because God has created us for them..

Good Works?

God has created us for good works. We do not do good works in order to gain more acceptance, love, or blessings from God. Instead, we work *from* all these things, not *for* them. The good works we do bring glory and honor to God, but are more about others, than God. Put another way, good works are about loving others, not necessarily pleasing God.

Of course, God is pleased and delighted when we choose to trust Him and do the good works He has prepared for us. Ephesians 2:10 says,

> For we are his workmanship, created in Christ Jesus for good works, which God prepared beforehand, that we should walk in them.

Some translations say that we are His "masterpiece." Do not miss the order here. We do not do good works to become God's masterpiece. Since we are God's master-piece, we are designed for good works. It's the most fulfilling thing we can do. We're created in Christ for good works.

Our place in Christ is also the motivation for our good works. Christ in us is more than enough to motivate and inspire us to live godly. He's not motivating us by promising future jewels or square footage. No, He motivates us by teaching us who we are and what we really want.

God also gives us more than enough grace to do the things He calls us to do (2 Corinthians 9:8). The important thing to remember is God loves you without condition. And your position in Christ is not affected in any way by what you do for Him. Further, we're saved by grace, not by works (Ephesians 2:8-9). So our works are *from* grace, not *for* grace.

When we do good works, we get the amazing opportunity to participate in God's work in this world. It's a privilege and honor. God does not need us to do good works in order to accomplish His plans. Instead, God invites us into these good works so that we can enjoy Him by loving others.

So we can freely do good works from a "want to" motivation, not a "have to" motivation based on fear. It is God's love, not His fear, that motivates us (2 Corinthians 5:14).

Do Works Save Us?

Many people quote James 2:17, faith without works is dead, to try to argue that we need works in order to be saved. I believe when we look at how James defines faith and works, we'll see the liberating truth of what James is trying to communicate.

It's worth noting how Scripture shouts to us that we are saved by grace alone through faith alone. We are made right, freely by grace through faith (Romans 3:23, 5:1; Titus 3:7); we have eternal life by believing in Jesus (John 3:16; Romans 3:22, 10:9-10); we are not justified by works (Galatians 2:16, 3:5-8); and we have a right standing with God that comes by faith (Philippians 3:9; Galatians 2:21; Romans 4:5).

If our salvation was based on works, then how many works would it take? Not only that, but Romans 3:12 says no one does good. And Isaiah 64:6 says all our works are like filthy rags. Clearly we cannot be saved by what we do, since what we do is no good.

I believe that James is not talking about many works that we do over the period of our life, but what real faith looks like. To James, real faith is a faith that chooses to trust Jesus—unlike the fake "faith" of the demons who believe only that there's a God (James 2:19). The difference between the believer and the demon is that the believer chooses to trust Jesus to save him, while the demon merely believes there is one God while refusing to trust Jesus for salvation.

James tells us what he means by faith without works is dead. In verse 21, James says Abraham was justified by works when he offered up his son Isaac. Is this right? What does James mean by works? Paul tells us that Abraham was *not* justified by works (Romans 4:2), but was justified by faith (Romans 4:3). Therefore, James must mean something else by works. This is why in verse 23, James clarifies himself by saying what Paul said, "Abraham believed God…"

Abraham offered his son only one time, and to James, this is called *works*. This is crucial. For James, 'faith with works' means choosing Jesus and letting Him save you. Jesus said the work of God is to believe in the One He sent (John 6:29). Sometimes the biblical writers will use the word *work* or *works* to simply describe living faith.

James goes on to say that Rahab was justified by works "when she received the messengers and sent them out by another way" (James 2:25). How many times did she open the door to receive the messengers? One time. And this one act is called "works" by James.

When Jesus knocked on the door of our hearts, we opened it by faith and let Him in one time, and we were saved. Therefore James sees works as a one-time response to the gospel.[18]

In summary, dead faith (faith without works) is a faith that does not choose to let Jesus save. Faith with works (living faith) is faith that chooses to let Jesus save. Put another way, dead faith merely acknowledges that there's a God, but living faith chooses to let God save. Though stated in plural form, the "works" James describes is really the one work of believing in Jesus.

Don't Freak Out

Am I doing enough? Do I have the works? Is God pleased? All those questions can be put to rest when we realize that

God does not need us. He does not need our good works, nor does He need us to do tasks for Him.

Nevertheless, God wants us. He wants to share His love and life with us. He does not want us to run around doing things for Him and miss Him in it all. He wants *you for you*, not what you can do for Him. Yes, you can please Him through what you do. But He's already pleased with who you are. So we get to live from His delight, not for it.

Jesus is enough. His work on your behalf is enough. There's no need for you to worry about what you do for God. He has your good works planned out (Ephesians 2:10). Your job is to just be available and walk in them. His life within you will motivate you and inspire you.

Enjoy Jesus. Enjoy His smile on you all day. And be confident that He is pleased with you.

CHAPTER 16

Obedience and Status

Every believer wants to obey God because God has put this new desire in our heart (Romans 6:17). It's part of our new identity (1 Peter 1:14). However, it's not our obedience to God that makes us righteous. Instead, it was Jesus's obedience to God that made us righteous (Romans 5:19). It's important to understand that we obey God because He has already saved, accepted, blessed, and secured us. We do not obey for these things.

Paul says that our obedience is actually a fruit of our trust in Christ. He calls it the "obedience of faith" (Romans 1:5, 16:26). Put simply, our trust in Christ is our obedience. When we trust in Christ, we're obeying Him and allowing Him to live His life through us. Of course, this is not passive, but active. We choose to trust Christ in every moment. And by this choice, we automatically walk by the Spirit.

Jesus gave us a new command to love one another even as He has loved us (John 13:34). And 1 John 5:3 reminds us that God's commands are not burdensome. I say this because we aren't told to follow the Ten Commandments or any of the law. We've been set free from the law so that we can live under God's grace (Romans 6:14).

We do not need an external guide (the law), since we now have the eternal Guide living in us. Jesus's life in us is more than enough to bring about obedience. Jesus is not asking us to obey the law or try and keep the law. He's asking that we get to know His love so we can love one another. His yoke is easy and His burden is light (Matthew 11:30).

Greatest and Least in the Kingdom?

If we are all perfect in heaven and all got there because of grace, then how can there be some "greater" than others? Some have taken Jesus's teaching on the greatest and least in the kingdom as a way of motivating Christians to work hard so they can earn more responsibility or status in God's kingdom. But in context, we shall see that it's not about status one day in heaven, but about Jesus's way of grace.

Jesus says in Matthew 11:11:

> Truly I say to you, among those born of women there has not arisen anyone greater than John the Baptist! Yet the one who is least in the kingdom of heaven is greater than he.

Jesus clearly isn't talking believers outperforming John the Baptist, since no one is greater than John the Baptist. John the Baptist was a prophet under the old covenant and did not have the chance to participate in the new covenant. That's why "the least" here refers to any believer who has called on Jesus under the new covenant.

The least are given the same status as those who were great in the old covenant. That's the point here. Jesus is reversing the way we understand those who are great and those who are least.

Jesus's way of grace means that we're all on equal footing, no matter how great we lived. All get treated the same because it's all by grace. In other places, Jesus refers to the greatest in the kingdom as being those who simply believe in Him and do what He says (Matthew 18:4; Luke 9:48). Further, in most cases, He's referring to participating right now in God's kingdom.

Some will say that those who do more good will gain more responsibility in heaven. They cite Matthew 19:28, where Jesus promises the disciples that they will judge Israel. However, this text is directed to the disciples and no one else. Nonetheless, all believers are told that we will judge the world and angels (1 Corinthians 6:2-3). So this special responsibility in Matthew 19:28 is not special at all. Further, it's not a hierarchy that lasts for eternity, but something that's done one time.

The verses these teachers use to proof-text always have in view all believers, not some. Further, those who teach that we can gain more responsibility or status miss the concept that we are saved by grace, kept by grace, and brought to heaven by grace alone. It's all a gift from God. We are all made perfect and saved by grace alone. Therefore, our status before God is the same.

All One In Christ

I am God's favorite. And so are you. We're all equal in Christ (Galatians 3:28). This means we aren't competing with one another. We're all on the same team. We all have the same position and status with God.

We are all saved by grace. And all of us will be able to boast only in Christ, not in what we did. This is important because it frees us to enjoy Christ and Christ in others. We do not need to feel pressure to have it all together, or to fake it around others. We're all the same. We're all on equal ground.

Our total forgiveness means that we're free to be ourselves. We don't have to impress others. We don't have to seek after acceptance or love from others, since we are fully accepted and loved by God.

The race of the Christian life is not for the prize of beating others. The prize is Christ. And the race is about enjoying Him and enjoying the gift of relationships along the way.

REASON 3

YOUR GOD IS GOOD

CHAPTER 17

You Cannot Lose Your Salvation

One of the most debated topics in Christianity is whether or not believers can lose their salvation. I'm going to make the case based on the overwhelming biblical evidence, that believers cannot lose their salvation. Salvation is a gift from God based on His work for us. Our salvation is not about us, our promise, or our faithfulness. Our salvation is based on God's promise, work, and faithfulness to us.

New Covenant

In order to understand our eternal security, we have to realize the agreement God made with Himself. Yes, Himself. God swears by Himself in order to keep His promise (Hebrews 6:16-18). This is in contrast to the old covenant where the covenant was between God and humanity. The old covenant was about humanity's faithfulness to God, but they were terrible at this (Hebrews 8:8-9).

So God came in and fixed the problem by taking humanity out of the equation. Now instead of an agreement (covenant) between God and man, the covenant is between God and God, and we are the heirs to the promise (Hebrews 6:17). An inheritance is given freely because we're a part of the family. That's why salvation is not earned but given freely through faith.

This is also why salvation is purely based on grace, and not on what we do or don't do. And anyone who thinks they can lose their salvation always thinks that they have the power to do it. But our salvation is not in our hands. We did not have the power to earn or effect our salvation, and we do not have the power to lose it. Our salvation is directly tied to the covenant we are under. Since our salvation is based on God's promise to himself, we can be confident that we will be saved forever.

Salvation is not about our faithfulness to God, but His faithfulness to us. That is what's so different about the new covenant. It's not about us, but about God's promise to Himself that He will be our God and will remember our sins no more (Hebrews 8:10-12).

Eternal Life

Now that we've laid the foundation, let's look at passages that speak of the security we have in Christ. We'll see that God gives us eternal life, not temporary life. Our security rests in God's hand, not ours; God's strength, not ours.

Once we're saved, we're placed in Christ. This position in Christ means that nothing can separate us from His love, nothing can snatch us from His hand, and nothing can cause Him to leave us:

> For I am convinced that neither death, nor life, nor angels, nor principalities, nor things present, nor things to come, nor powers, nor height, nor depth, nor any other created thing, will be able to separate us from the love of God, which is in Christ Jesus our Lord. (Romans 8:38-39)

> I give them eternal life, and they will *never* perish, and *no one* will snatch them out of my hand. (John 10:28)

> I will *never* desert you, nor will I *ever* forsake you. (Hebrews 13:5)

Your sins have been taken away once and for all. So what is the one thing that could have taken you out of God's hand? *Sin.* But what did Jesus do with our sin? *He took it away forever!* That's why it's foolish to think we can lose our salvation.

Our salvation is eternal. This means it lasts forever. God does not say we have temporal life that could be lost. God wants us to know we have eternal life. He wants us to know that we're safe forever:

> Whoever believes will in Him have eternal life. For God so loved the world, that He gave His only begotten Son, that whoever believes in Him shall not perish, but have *eternal* life. (John 3:15-16 NASB)

> These things I have written to you who believe in the name of the Son of God, so that you may know that you have *eternal* life. (1 John 5:13 NASB)

> Therefore He is able also to *save forever* those who draw near to God through Him. (Hebrews 7:25 NASB)

> He has caused us to be born again to a living hope through the resurrection of Jesus Christ from the dead, to an inheritance that is *imperishable*, undefiled, and unfading, kept in heaven for you, who by God's power are being guarded through faith for a salvation ready to be revealed in the last time. (1 Peter 1:3-5 NASB)

Not only is our salvation eternal, but God promises to save us forever, no matter what. He promises to guard us and protect us. And He promises that our inheritance is imperishable and will not fade away. We can know and have confidence that we are saved, because our salvation is in God's hands.

For this reason, the Scriptures tell us that we are destined for heaven, already seated in heaven, and already have our citizenship there. There's no doubt in the New Testament that believers are safe and secure:

> Rejoice that your names are recorded in heaven.
> (Luke 10:20 NASB)

> For our citizenship is in heaven, from which also we eagerly wait for a Savior, the Lord Jesus Christ.
> (Philippians 3:20 NASB)

> And raised us up with him and seated us with him in the heavenly places in Christ Jesus. (Ephesians 2:6)

Can it get any clearer? We are headed where we're already seated spiritually. God is not going to kick us out of heaven. He loves us and wants us to know that we already have the best place in heaven reserved for us—His right hand!

God has sealed us. He has promised that He will save us until the end. He will finish what He started in us. And He will be faithful to us no matter how unfaithful we are to Him. It's by God's work and love that we're saved, and it will continue to be by God's work and love that we stay saved:

> In him you also, when you heard the word of truth, the gospel of your salvation, and believed in him, were *sealed* with the promised Holy Spirit. (Ephesians 1:13 NASB)

> Do not grieve the Holy Spirit of God, by whom you were *sealed* for the day of redemption. (Ephesians 4:30 NASB)

> For I am confident of this very thing, that He who began a good work in you *will perfect it* until the day of Christ Jesus. (Philippians 1:6)

> If we are faithless, He *remains* faithful, for He cannot deny Himself. (2 Timothy 2:13 NASB)

> Now to him who is able to *keep you* from stumbling and to present you blameless before the presence of his glory with great joy. (Jude 24 NASB)

Now He who establishes us with you in Christ and anointed us is God, who also *sealed* us and gave us the Spirit in our hearts as a pledge. (2 Corinthians 1:21-22)

It's the word of God, not my opinion, that affirms the truth that we're saved once and for all. We are safe in God's hand. We are secure. There's nothing you can do to change that. All the questions related to our sins are not a factor, because Jesus has taken away all our big and little sins, and He promises to save us forever.

In regard to your salvation, the cross worked. The cross is enough. You are saved! You can be confident in your salvation because your God is good, faithful, and will never let you go.

CHAPTER 18

You Cannot Fall Away

You cannot fall away, be thrown away, or walk away from your salvation. Nothing can separate you from God's love. And nothing can cause you to lose what Jesus has freely given you. Just like your physical birth, once you've been born again in Christ, you cannot be "unborn." Your salvation is irreversible.

A passage in Matthew 7 has led many believers to doubt whether they're saved. Jesus is teaching there about how to tell a false teacher from a true one (Matthew 7:15). He then contrasts good trees bearing good fruit, and bad trees bearing bad fruit (7:16-20). He's not saying we're saved by our fruit; He's revealing that someone who is not saved cannot bear good fruit.

Then He says not everyone who says "Lord, Lord" will enter the kingdom, but he who does the will of the Father will enter (7:21). He is contrasting dead faith and living faith, just as James does. What is the *will* of the Father?

John 6:40 says, "For this is the will of My Father, that everyone who beholds the Son and believes in Him will have eternal life."

So there will be some who acknowledge Jesus as God and Lord, like the demons do, but who do not believe in Him to save them. That's why Jesus will declare to them He never knew them (7:23). He's talking to those who are false prophets, who practice lawlessness, and who don't believe in Jesus as Savior. These people were using Jesus in order to perform miracles (7:22) but were doing it for personal gain. They did not do the will of the Father, which was to simply believe in His Son, Jesus.

If you believe in Christ, then He knows you. He loves you. And He will never disown you.

Fall Away?

Some quote Hebrews 6 in order to say that believers can fall away or walk away from their salvation. But as always, context is our friend. And we'll see that Hebrews 6:4-8 is not talking to those who are saved.

We know this because right after Hebrews 6:4-8, the writer says, "But, beloved, we are convinced of better things concerning you, and things that accompany salvation, though we are speaking in this way."

Hebrews 6:4-6 says that these people who fell away were once enlightened, tasted the heavenly gift, partook of the Holy Spirit, and tasted the word of God—and that it's impossible to renew them again to repentance because they "crucify to themselves the Son of God and put Him to open shame" (6:6).

The writer then contrasts believers and unbelievers in verses 7-8 by saying there are two kinds of ground. A ground that drinks the rain, and a ground that does not. The first ground receives a blessing, the other ground is burned up.

The whole point of this passage is that there are some who try out Jesus, but never believe in His sacrifice. These people have rejected Christ and His sacrifice. There are many people who hear the gospel, participate in a church experience, experience the love and grace of God, but reject Jesus as the way to be saved.

Thrown Away?

In John 15, Jesus once again is contrasting the benefits of those who abide in Him and those who do not. "Abide" is not something that believers do occasionally. We abide (live) in Christ at all times. So abiding is not a work for us to maintain; instead, it's our location. It's a fact. Believers abide (live) in Christ.[19]

This is why Jesus says that anyone who does not abide (live) in Him is thrown away (John 15:6). This whole context is talking about the benefits of living in Christ. Apart from Christ, we can do nothing (John 15:5). This is why we should choose to live in Christ so that we can bear fruit.

Notice that we simply bear the fruit. A branch does not struggle or toil to bear fruit. No, we are not the source. Jesus, as our vine, is the source of our fruit. We simply get to show it off. That's the life of the believer: showing off Jesus to the world.

Work Out Your Salvation?

We're told to *work out* our salvation (Philippians 2:12), but we aren't told to *work for* our salvation. Big difference. God has begun a good work in us (Philippians 1:6). And we're now told to work out what God has worked in. This simply means to live out and express Christ. Be who God has made us to be. Do not stand around and do nothing. But live out your salvation.

We're not alone in this work. Since we're united with Christ, He is working in us and through us. He is helping us work out our salvation. That's why Philippians 2:13 says, "For it is God who is at work in you, both to will and to work for His good pleasure." That's the dynamic of the Christian life: our living and Jesus living through us are the same thing, since we're in union with Him. We work out our salvation by trusting the One who is working in us and through us.

CHAPTER 19

You're Not Lukewarm

In Revelation 3, we see that Jesus calls the church of Laodicea "lukewarm." As we'll see in this passage, there's no such thing as a lukewarm Christian. To be lukewarm is to not be saved.

The church of Laodicea was between two cities, Hierapolis and Colossae. The hot waters of Hierapolis had a medicinal (hot tub) effect and the cold waters of Colossae were pure, drinkable, and had a life-giving effect.[20] Laodicea didn't have a water source and had to get their water piped from surrounding springs. The problem is, once the water arrived in Laodicea, it was lukewarm and disgusting from the distance and the minerals in the pipe.[21] Therefore, Laodicea became well known for its lukewarm and disgusting water.[22]

Understanding that, we can conclude that this passage isn't trying to get lukewarm Christians to get "on fire for God." That's why Jesus said, I wish you were cold or hot (3:15). This implies that being cold is good and being hot is good. Therefore, being lukewarm means not to be saved.

The church at Laodicea was lukewarm, which meant they were not good for anything. Spiritually they were dead! This view fits in context because we aren't saved or accepted by whether we're on fire for God. We're saved and accepted by grace through faith. So if this passage is not about being on fire for God, what is it saying?

In verse 17, Jesus says that although they think they are rich and prosperous, in reality they're wretched, poor, blind, and naked. The same thought is found in Matthew 23:27, when Jesus condemns the Pharisees by comparing them to whitewashed tombs, beautiful on the outside but dead inside.

Yes, these people in Laodicea are spoken of as a church, but they're a church who profess Christ although not all believe in Christ. The church of Laodicea is filled with hypocritical Pharisees. This church is filled with self-righteous people who, like the Pharisees, trust not in Christ but in their own righteousness for salvation. In Revelation 3:18, Jesus asks them if He can anoint their eyes so that they can see. They are spiritually blind and cannot see their self-righteousness and hypocrisy.

How do I know Revelation 3:15-16 is to non-believers? Verse 20 reads:

> Behold, I stand at the door and knock. If anyone hears my voice and opens the door, I will come in to him and eat with him, and he with me.

We can see that they haven't opened the door and let Christ into their lives. Those of us who've trusted Christ for salvation have opened up the door and let Him in. This passage is dealing with self-righteous people who are not saved. They claim they know Christ but haven't trusted Him for salvation.

Jesus is warning this Pharisee-ridden church, that if they don't open the door of their hearts and let Him in (salvation), that come judgment day, He will spit them out (reject them).

Out of His love, He is calling them to be zealous and repent (3:19), to change their mind about their present sinful course of action. We know God loves all and wants all to come to repentance (2 Peter 3:9), which is why He's warning this church and wanting them to turn to Him to be saved.

So this verse is not about struggling Christians. Instead, it's about Jesus wanting these unbelieving Pharisees to come to repentance.

Blotted Out?

Some think that God will blot their name out of the book of life. This is due to a misunderstanding of Revelation 3:5, which says, "He who overcomes will thus be clothed in white garments; and I will not erase his name from the book of life."

This verse is meant to give us assurance, not fear, that God will keep us. God is not going to erase our name. We are safe and secure in Him. Further, 1 John 5:4-5 says that we who believe in Jesus are overcomers. All believers are overcomers, which means Revelation 3:5 is a promise from God, not a threat.

You can have confidence that God will never blot your name out of the book of life!

CHAPTER 20

The Truth about God's Discipline

In light of our total forgiveness and freedom from God's condemnation, what does God's discipline look like? As we journey through the book of Hebrews and the rest of the New Testament, we'll discover a radical truth: God's discipline is *not* punishment. God's discipline is about teaching us for what lies ahead.

For Our Good

I used to think that discipline was punishment for what I did. Growing up, when I would do something wrong, I would get spanked and grounded. Consequently, when I entered into relationship with my heavenly Father, I thought He was doing the same thing. I thought His discipline was punishment for my sins.

Just like forgiveness, we cannot compare how we do

things with how God does things. God teaches us and guides us without punishing us for our sins. We are always under God's discipline. God's discipline is His constant teaching, guidance, and instruction for us. He uses everything in our life to bring us to conformity to His Son (Romans 8:28-30).

God is not a hypocrite. He is not going to take away our sins and promise to never remember them, and then discipline us for them. That's not how He works. He's not punishing us for our sin. The punishment for our sin was death. And Jesus died. Now there's no condemnation for our sin (Romans 8:1). This means that God is not going to condemn us or punish us for our past, present, or future sins.

Hebrews 12 offers us the best picture of what God's discipline looks like in our life. The writer says that God disciplines those He loves (Hebrews 12:6), for our good (12:10), so that it "yields the peaceful fruit of righteousness" (Hebrews 12:11).

Furthermore, God disciplines us so that we can share in His holiness (12:10). This means that when God trains us, we get the amazing opportunity to participate in the very nature and character of God. God is not disciplining us so that we can become more holy in our identity. Instead, His discipline is about teaching us to live out of who we already are.

I was a football player in high school and college. And in the off-season, we would train ourselves to become stronger and faster. We were disciplining ourselves to become the best we could be. There were many days when this training was not joyful. But I knew that no matter how I felt in a given moment, the training would pay off.

In the same way, the writer tells us that sometimes discipline can seem sorrowful (Hebrews 12:11). This does not mean God is punishing us. Instead, we all go through difficult times and even in the most difficult times, God is teaching us and training us for what lies ahead. The writer moves on to say that after our training, it will yield the peaceful fruit of righteousness (12:11).

When God trains us, He teaches us to say no to sin and yes to the godly people He has made us (Titus 2:12). And as we learn to trust Him, we bear His fruit. We get to participate in His life and righteousness. When we bear His fruit, we express Him.

We are God's image bearers. When people see us, they see a picture of God. We've been re-created in His image and get the amazing opportunity to let Christ express Himself to the world through each one of us.

God loves us without condition. And He cares about

everything we do because He wants what's good for us. We see God's perspective on discipline when He commands human fathers to be like him:

> Fathers, do not provoke your children to anger, but bring them up in the discipline and instruction of the Lord. (Ephesians 6:4 NASB)

God is not provoking us to anger, either! He is not punishing us or making us mad, nor is He hurling insults our way for our bad behavior. He is patient and kind, and keeps no record of our wrongs (1 Corinthians 13:4-6).

God is not disgusted with you, nor is He impatient with your growth. There's no rush. And there are no expectations. The same God who saved us is the same God who will grow us, guide us, and lead us to live out of who we are in Him.

Circumstances

God is good. It's who He is. He cannot cease to be good. If He did, He would cease to be God. God is also love. It's who He is at the deepest level. Everything He does is because He is love. Knowing this will help us interpret our circumstances.

We all have bad circumstances; but it's important to

know that God is not the author of pain, suffering, or the evil of this world. The bad circumstances we face are not due to God punishing us for our sin. God is for us, not against us (Romans 8:31).

Life happens. Due to humanity's free will, bad things happen; but God is not behind these bad things. He does not cause evil or suffering. He allows it, but He does not cause it. He allowed free choice so that we can freely choose to be in relationship with Him because love is not forced. And in order for us to have a true relationship with God, He gave us the choice to accept His offer or reject it.

There is good news. One day, God will rid this world of all the evil and pain in it. And there's good news now. Christ in you is enough. He's enough to bring peace to you in the midst of your crazy circumstance. Although He does not promise to deliver us from our circumstance, He does promise to be life to us, no matter the circumstance.

Our suffering cannot rob us of what we have in Christ. If we already have everything we need in and through Christ, then suffering reveals to us how sufficient Christ really is. We do not need perfect circumstances in order to experience peace, happiness, or satisfaction. We have Christ, who is our peace, happiness, and satisfaction, and He is enough.

CHAPTER 21

God's Will

God's will is not a secret step-by-step plan. It's not a mystery we have to figure out. God's will is straightforward and simple. Before we look at what Scripture says is God's will, remember this—you are right with God and forgiven.

Our righteousness and forgiveness does not come from doing everything right. Our righteousness is given to us because Jesus did everything right on our behalf. And our forgiveness is solely based on Jesus and His shed blood.

This means that God's attitude toward us is not affected by how well we perform. His presence in us is always there. His love for us is never ending. And His grace will never run dry.

God's will is His desire. When you think of the word *will*, do not think of a detailed plan but think of desire. This is what *will* means. The will of God is His desire for our life. And we can understand and know God's will (Ephesians 5:17).

God's will is that we rejoice, pray, and give thanks:

> Rejoice always; pray without ceasing; in everything give thanks; for this is God's will for you in Christ Jesus. (1 Thessalonians 5:16-18)

We can rejoice in what God has done for us, in what God has done to us, and in what God is doing through us. Further, God wants us to talk to Him. The instruction "Pray without ceasing" does not mean every second of every day. It means God desires for us to speak to Him because He loves to hear about everything we're going through and doing.

And He desires that we give thanks in everything, not for everything. He's not asking that we give thanks for our bad circumstances or for the bad things that may happen to us. No, He's saying that we can give thanks in everything because in everything, we have all that we need in Him.

God's will is that we do what is right and pleasing to Him:

> Equip you in every good thing to do His will, working in us that which is pleasing in His sight, through Jesus Christ. (Hebrews 13:21 NASB)

> For such is the will of God that by doing right you may silence the ignorance of foolish men. (1 Peter 2:15)

God's desire is that we live out of who He has made us.

Why? Because the opposite of this would be to live in sin. God knows what's best for us and wants us to be fulfilled by walking after Him.

Here's the cool thing. We can please God by what we do. He delights in us every time we trust Him and express His Son. Not only does He delight in who we are, but He also delights in what we do in dependence of Him.

However, our sin and bad behavior never makes God displeased with who we are. Everything that isn't pleasing to God, He has forgiven and forgotten. So we cannot make God mad through what we do, since we are not what we do.

Remember, He separates our identity from our behavior. And His attitude toward us is not based on what we do, but on who He has made us.

God's will is for all people to believe, be saved, and come to repentance:

> Who desires all men to be saved and to come to the knowledge of the truth. (1 Timothy 2:4)

> The Lord is not slow about His promise, as some count slowness, but is patient toward you, not wishing for any to perish but for all to come to repentance. (2 Peter 3:9)

> For this is the will of my Father, that everyone who looks on the Son and believes in him should have

eternal life, and I will raise him up on the last day. (John 6:40)

I love God's heart. He wants everyone to be saved. And He's pursuing everyone with His reckless love. He truly loves the world (John 3:16). And He loves you. We can trust in the character of God because His character is love.

God's desire for us is to look to His Son and believe in Him. God's desire for us is to not be overwhelmed by our sins or our circumstances. Instead, He wants us to gaze at His Son, the one who has taken away our sins. God's will is that we look to Jesus in every moment, knowing that He is enough.

Always Within You

Sure, there are times when we do not live out God's desire for us. This is called sin. But when we sin, we aren't somehow messing up what God wants to do through us and for us.

We're all faced with tough decisions in life. And we all ask the same question: What is God's will? In these moments, God wants us to use wisdom and to talk with trusted friends. No matter what job or car you choose, God is within you.

Ask God for wisdom and know that He is with you no matter what you choose. The same is true for a job or for your bowl of cereal each morning. God has given us freedom to choose. And He is saying that no matter what we choose, He is within us and for us.

That's the great thing about God's will. You can do it anywhere. His will is essentially to love others. Put another way, His will for your life is to trust Jesus. So you can do that at either house. You can do that at the job in New York or in California. No matter where you go or what you choose, Christ is in you.

You can have confidence in every moment because God is within you, no matter what.

CHAPTER 22

It Is Finished!

After a long week of work and school, I went home to visit my parents and little brother, Christian. I was looking forward to sleeping in that Saturday, but Christian had other plans. He ran into my room at 6:00 a.m. that Saturday morning, yelling, "Bubba, bubba, wake up! It's family day!" I was thinking, *Family day? I don't care about family day. Let me go back to sleep!*

Of course, I didn't go back to sleep. Who could, when someone that cute is giving you cuddles and wants to play? Next thing I knew, he convinced me to take him to the mall, where all I remember is playing outside on a rock wall. (Doesn't everyone go to the mall to play on a rock wall in the parking lot?) Christian wanted to jump off a five-foot rock wall into my arms. So of course, I let him do it. I put him up there and he jumped, and I caught him. He loved it. We did this time and time again. He was laughing and having an amazing time. And I was loving the fact that he was jumping into my arms with full confidence.

Do you see that? Christian trusted who I was. He knew I would never drop him. He wanted to trust me. His only concern in that moment was to have fun while trusting me.

We can have confidence in our heavenly Father because He loves us, cares for us, and will never drop us. We can boldly run into His throne of grace, even early in the morning. He wants us to bother Him. He loves it. He loves us. And nothing can change that.

We don't need to have any other concerns, because Jesus has fully forgiven us, accepted us, and saved us. We get to simply enjoy Jesus in every moment.

It is done. It is finished. All the work that needed to be done to make you forgiven, cleansed, and close to God, was done by Christ on your behalf. There's no need to run around and try to do what has already been done. God has seated you with Christ. So are you resting with Him in His finished work?

No matter what you feel, no matter what you think, the cross is still enough. Jesus is still enough. And what He did for you is still true. His love will never run out on you. He will never leave you. He cannot love you less than He does now. And He promises that in every struggle, in every pain, in every doubt, He'll be there.

The cross worked for you. In every moment, you can have confidence that God loves you, is within you, is for you, and will never leave you!

Thank you, Jesus!

NOTES

Chapter 1

[1] For *saints* in the New Testament, see: Rom. 1:7, 8:27, 12:13, 15:25; 1 Cor. 1:2; 2 Cor. 1:1; Eph. 1:1; Phil. 1:1; Col. 1:2. For *holy*, see: 1 Cor. 3:17; Eph. 1:4; Col. 1:22. For *sanctified*, see 1 Cor. 6:11. For *righteous*, see 2 Cor. 5:21.

Chapter 3

[2] Kruse, C. G. *The Letter of John* (Grand Rapids, MI; Leicester, England: Eerdmans, 2000.), 42.

[3] Farley, Andrew. *The Naked Gospel*. (Grand Rapids: Zondervan, 2009), 153.

[4] Kruse, 44.

[5] D. L. Akin, *1, 2, 3 John*. (Nashville: Broadman & Holman, 2001.), 74. This is an early form of Gnosticism.

[6] Kruse., 48.

[7] C. Haas, M. deJonge, and J. L. Swellengrebel, *A Handbook on the Letters of John*. (New York: United Bible Societies. 1994.), 30.

[8] Kruse., 53.

[9] Ibid., 68.

Chapter 5

[10] Farley, Andrew. *The Naked Gospel.* 159.

Chapter 6

[11] D. A. Carson, (1991). *The Gospel according to John* (Leicester, England; Grand Rapids, MI: Inter-Varsity Press; Eerdmans), 464.

Chapter 7

[12] P. Ellingworth, *The Epistle to the Hebrews: A Commentary on the Greek Text* (Grand Rapids, MI; Carlisle, Cumbria, UK: Eerdmans; Paternoster Press. 1993.), 490.

[13] Ibid.. 541.

Chapter 9

[14] Carson, D. A. (1991). *The Gospel according to John* (p. 538). Leicester, England; Grand Rapids, MI: Inter-Varsity Press; Eerdmans), 538.

[15] Farley, Andrew. *God Without Religion.* (Grand Rapids, MI: Baker Books), 203.

Chapter 11

[16] http://www.etsjets.org/files/JETS-PDFs/35/35-2/JETS_35-2_159-172_Blomberg.pdf

[17] Elwell, Walter A. "Entry for 'Crown'". "Evangelical Dictionary of Theology". 1997.

Chapter 15

[18] Farley, Andrew. *Relaxing with God.* (Grand Rapids, MI: Baker Books), 113.

Chapter 18

[19] Farley, Andrew. *The Naked Gospel.* 193.

Chapter 19

[20] Beale, G. K. (1999). *The Book of Revelation: A Commentary on the Greek Text* (Grand Rapids, MI; Carlisle, Cumbria, UK: Eerdmans; Paternoster), 303.

[21] J. F. Walvoord, *Revelation*, in J. F. Walvoord & R. B. Zuck (Eds.), The Bible Knowledge Commentary: An Exposition of the Scriptures *The Bible Knowledge Commentary: An Exposition of the Scriptures*, vol. 2, (Wheaton, IL: Victor, 1985) 940.

[22] P. Patterson, *Revelation* (E. R. Clendenen, Ed.) vol. 39 (Nashville, TN: Broadman & Holman, 2012).

This is not an endorsement of these authors. They are, however, scholars who are credible. Although I do not agree with everything they have written, they did provide helpful information to me.

STUDY GUIDE

Chapter 1 – Past, Present, and Future

1. Personally, what does it mean for you to be forgiven of all your sins?
2. How does your total forgiveness enable you to live with confidence?
3. How does our forgiveness help us see ourselves?
4. How does your total forgiveness help you deal with your past?

Chapter 2 – Nothing Left to Forgive

1. Why is it so hard to believe we are totally forgiven?
2. Why does our total forgiveness not make us want to sin more?
3. Why can't believers commit the unforgiveable sin?

Chapter 3 – 1 John 1:9

1. Is 1 John 1:9 a verse for believers?
2. How does verses 8 and 10 help us understand the true context of 1 John 1:9?
3. Why is confession of sins to others and God healthy?

Chapter 4 – Fellowship with God

1. Do believers go in and out of fellowship with God?
2. How does God's presence help us with loneliness?
3. Are believers "growing closer to God"?

Chapter 5 – The Lord's Prayer

1. How does understanding the starting place of the new covenant help us interpret Jesus' teachings?
2. How does our once for all forgiveness change the way we pray?
3. How does our total forgiveness change the way we see God?

Chapter 6 – Two Kinds of Forgiveness?

1. God is not disappointed with you. Discuss what this means to you.
2. How does knowing you are pure help you with your past?
3. How does recognizing God's voice help us deal with shame?

Chapter 7 – You Cannot Out Sin God's Grace

1. Why is it beneficial to hear and speak truth into other's lives?
2. How does confessing our sins to one another bring healing?

3. Do believers sin willfully?

4. What does God think of you?

Chapter 8 – What Happens When We Sin?

1. What is repentance? And why is it good for the believer?

2. Why is sorrow and regret over sin a good thing?

3. Are you in the Spirit when you sin?

Chapter 9 – Conviction and Communion

1. Does the Holy Spirit convict believers?

2. What is the Holy Spirit doing in our lives?

3. What is the unworthy manner?

Chapter 10 – No More Tears

1. How do you picture judgment day?

2. Will believers be judged for their sins?

3. What does it mean to be blameless?

Chapter 11 – Jesus is our Reward

1. Is Jesus enough or do we need more to motivate us?

2. How will believers be treated on the Day of Judgment?

3. And how does knowing we will be treated like Jesus give

you confidence?

4. How does your confidence before God on judgment day give you confidence today?

Chapter 12 – No More Fear

1. Why is hard to believe that God is for us?
2. Why is fear of death removed when we understand God's love?
3. How does knowing we are loved and forgiven cast out fear?

Chapter 13 – Judgment By Works?

1. What is our motivation for good works?
2. Why does God judge our works?
3. What happens to our bad works?

Chapter 14 – God Is Not An Accountant

1. What does it mean to give an account to God?
2. Why won't we be judged for every bad word we say?
3. God does not need you but wants you. How does this change the way you relate to God and live your life?

Chapter 15 – Faith Without Works

1. Do we have to do good works in order for God to love

and accept us?

2. What is "works" according to James? And why can no one be saved through the good works they do?

3. God wants you for who you are, not what you can do for Him. Why is this an important distinction to make?

Chapter 16 – Obedience and Status

1. Why should we obey God?

2. God's love and acceptance of you is not based on your obedience. Discuss why obeying from your acceptance is important to know.

3. No matter how much we have failed or succeeded – we all have the same status. Discuss why this frees us to be ourselves.

Chapter 17 – You Cannot Lose Your Salvation

1. What is the New Covenant?

2. Why can nothing take us from God's hand or separate us from God's love?

3. How does being seated in heaven change your perspective on your current circumstances?

Chapter 18 – You Cannot Fall Away

1. What does it mean to abide in Christ?

2. What does it mean to work out your salvation?

3. Discuss this thought: since you are united to Christ, being yourself and letting Christ live through you is the same thing.

Chapter 19 – You're Not Lukewarm

1. Why can't believers be lukewarm?

2. Your name is written in the book of life. How does this make you feel?

Chapter 20 – The Truth About God's Discipline

1. What does God's discipline look like?

2. Why is God's discipline not a reaction to our sin?

3. God's discipline is not punishment for your sins. How does this change the way you understand God's discipline?

Chapter 21 – God's Will

1. What is God's will?

2. Does God bless us based on how well we live?

3. God is within you no matter what you choose. How does this freedom help you make decisions?

Chapter 22 – It Is Finished!

1. What characteristic of God allows you to trust Him?
2. What does "It is Finished" mean for you personally?
3. What does it mean to rest in Christ?

ACKNOWLEDGMENTS

Writing this book is a dream come true. I want to firstly thank my Savior—Jesus Christ. Thank you for giving me the strength and words to make this book happen.
I want to thank my entire family who has prayed for and supported me my entire life. I love you all so much and I pray the truth in this book becomes the banner you all live under.

I want to thank everyone who gave me feedback and support during the writing process. Your words, feedback, criticism, and encouragement helped make this book way better than I could have imagined. Especially my church, Church Without Religion. Thank you all for the encouragement and support. I am so thankful I get to serve you!

I want to think my pastor, friend, and theological hero, Drew Farley. Thank you for all your support, guidance, and training over the past few years.

I want to specifically thank everyone who made this book become a reality by supporting me financially. Thank you, Jerod Clopton, Matt McMillen, Randy Hofer, Kathy Wilkinson, Marie Robinson, Cris Corzine-McCloskey, Kathy Rasnake, Glenn Webb, Dana Hodges, Kyle Butler,

Tyson Snow, Tony Sutherland, Stacey Smith, Sam Wheat, David Blazer, Wynema Clark, Lee Higginbotham, Richard Yager, Sheena Bryant, Marcia Bishoff, Sandra Campbell, Robin Fondurulia, and Silas Jones.

And last but certainly not least, I want to thank the Kennedy Family for their support, love, and encouragement during this entire process. You all are such a gift from God and I am so thankful for you!

Zach Maldonado is a pastor, speaker, and author. His passion is to proclaim the gospel and to help people believe Jesus is enough. He holds a Master of Arts in Theology degree from Fuller Theological Seminary. Connect with Zach on Instagram, Twitter, and Facebook (@ZachMaldo). For messages and more information visit **ZachMaldonado.org**

INTERESTED IN HAVING ZACH SPEAK AT YOUR CHURCH OR EVENT?

Visit the speaking page at
Zachmaldonado.org to send an inquiry